TREVOR MERRIDEN

IRRESISTIBLE
FORCES

the business legacy of **Napster** & the
growth of the **Underground Internet**

CAPSTONE

First published 2001 by
Capstone Publishing Limited (A Wiley Company)
8 Newtec Place
Magdalen Road
Oxford OX4 1RE
United Kingdom
http://www.capstoneideas.com

CIP catalogue records for this book are available from the British Library
and the US Library of Congress

ISBN 1-84112-170-3

Typeset in 11/16 pt Bodoni Book by
Sparks Computer Solutions Ltd, Oxford, UK
http://www.sparks.co.uk
Printed and bound by
T.J. International Ltd, Padstow, Cornwall

This book is printed on acid-free paper

Substantial discounts on bulk quantities of Capstone books are available to corporations, professional associations and other organizations. For details telephone Capstone Publishing on (+44-1865-798623), fax (+44-1865-240941) or e-mail info@wiley-capstone.com

To Melanie.

With your love and support, you did more than anyone else
to make this book possible

Contents

Preface and Acknowledgments

THIS BOOK IS ABOUT – but not only about – Napster. The story of Napster is important in its own right, but perhaps its legacy is even more so. The music file sharing phenomenon, whatever its eventual fate, has highlighted the extraordinary potential for the mass mobilization of community and consumer power. It has also prompted many businesses to assess the commercial potential of what has become known as "peer-to-peer."

Napster's founder Shawn Fanning didn't invent file sharing. He didn't invent the wider concept of peer-to-peer networking. And he didn't even invent Napster totally on his own – the project was of course his but he got some valuable help from friends along the way. But Fanning knew early on what he wanted Napster to be. A friend who knew Fanning before Napster says "I'm pretty sure that Fanning just woke up with the idea one day that it would be neat if people could share their music with one another."

Fanning believed (as perhaps only a teenager could) that people would actually love to share what was theirs with one another. He found plenty of people who kept telling him that people would not be interested in a file sharing program. One hacker told him bluntly, "it's a selfish world and nobody wants to share." Yet Fanning's personal experiences led him to feel more upbeat about human nature. Even selfish people would be up for sharing, he reasoned, if only through a sense of enlightened self-interest. The feeling drove him on ... and on. Friends believe that he was driven to develop Napster more from a desire to prove to himself right on this point, rather than impress others with his technical mastery of programming language.

As we all know now, Fanning was right and the cynics were very, very wrong. Napster's reputation spread quickly and more people checked it out. And as more people checked it out, the range of available MP3s (online music files) became larger. And the larger the range, the more its reputation spread.

Just before a court ordered Napster to remove all materials infringing copyright early in 2001, one estimate put the number of users at around 58 million and the number may well have been higher if you believe some other estimates. Who were these people? All of us. Not just students, who became early Napster adopters through the luxury of wide bandwidth at their colleges and schools across the United States, but the 30-somethings, looking for their 1980s favorites, and then the 40-somethings checking out rare jazz records from Finland.

The rapid spread in Napster's popularity has made many business people sit up and take notice. Unfortunately for Napster, most of those noticing initially came from record labels. The messy court battles that have since halted Napster in its tracks have, nevertheless, served to alert people to their own community and consumer power, and other businesses to the wider commercial potential of file sharing and peer-to-peer networking.

Shawn Fanning himself recognized the wider potential of peer-to-peer. In a testimony before the Senate Judiciary Committee in Provo, Utah, on October 9, 2000, he said:

> *"I believe that the peer-to-peer technology on which Napster is based has the potential to be adopted for many different uses. People generally speak about the ability to share other kinds of files in addition to music, and indeed, Napster has been contacted by entities such as the Human Genome Project that are interested in sharing information among specific communities of interest. But peer-to-peer technology, or distributed computing, also has tremendous opportunity for sharing resources or computing power, lowering information and transaction costs. Peer-to-peer could be used to create a pool of resources in aggregate to solve a range of complex storage, processing and bandwidth problems. Peer-to-peer also has the potential to change today's understanding of the relationship between source and site. Think how much faster and more efficient the Internet could be if instead of always connecting you to a central server every time you click on to a web site, your computer would find the source that housed that information nearest to you – if it's already on the computer of the kid down the hall, why travel halfway around the*

world to retrieve it? A number of companies, from Intel on down to small start-ups, are looking at ways to develop peer-to-peer technology, and I believe that many of them will succeed."

Certainly the potential is there, as the large numbers of philanthropic and commercial projects highlighted in the later stages of this book show. These are finding ways of using the essential elements of peer-to-peer, file sharing, distributed computing, distributed search engines and even mobile devices in order to make money.

Here is a guide to the layout of this book.

CHAPTER 1: THE BIRTH OF THE NAPSTER PHENOMENON

This chapter highlights the extraordinary story of how Napster founder, Shawn Fanning, came to write the source code for a file sharing program that the world now knows as Napster.

CHAPTER 2: WHY NAPSTER SPREAD LIKE WILDFIRE

The force that drove Fanning on was a passionate belief that people really wanted to share music and opinions *en masse* via the Internet. This was a pretty cool idea but very many people, including many of his friends, doubted that enough people would want to share their record collections with complete strangers on the other side of the world. In the end they were all wrong and he was right. This chapter charts the rise of Napster to become the fastest-growing phenomenon on the Internet, signing up millions of users, spawning the growth of a massive underground Internet community.

CHAPTER 3: BIG BOYS GET ANGRY

This chapter looks at how the five major record labels, both individually and collectively through the Recording Industry Association of America (RIAA), alongside big name artists such as Metallica and Dr Dre, grew in their hostility to what they saw as Napster's attack on their copyright.

CHAPTER 4: THE BATTLE COMMENCES

With an array of powerful forces lined up against it, it was inevitable that sooner rather than later the lawyers would get involved. When the record companies ganged up on Napster, they simply tried to shut it down through the courts. They won their legal battles, but in the process only created greater awareness of Napster and the potential of file sharing and peer-to-peer networking for consumers and other areas of business.

CHAPTER 5: THE VOICE OF THE PEOPLE:
THE FURY OF THE UNDERGROUND INTERNET

Napster's drawn out destruction by the record companies infuriated music lovers, who had begun to enjoy the sense of empowerment that it gave them over big business. The wrath of millions of fans spread rapidly through the underground Internet.

CHAPTER 6: BERTELSMANN
(AND THE END OF NAPSTER AS WE KNOW IT)

Bertelsmann was notable by its absence from the debate over Napster. Some senior executives at Bertelsmann had begun to think the unthinkable: file sharing was obviously a success, just as Shawn Fanning had predicted. Some at Bertelsmann wanted to get to know Napster a lot better, rather than just fight it tooth and nail. The result was an announcement which at the time shook the business world.

CHAPTER 7: CHILDREN OF NAPSTER –
MUSIC AND VIDEO

Ultimately, technology cannot be ignored and many file sharing peer-to-peer startups tried to become neo-Napsters. This chapter charts the mixed fortunes of the children of Napster – the offshoot upstarts such as Aimster, Flycode, Launch Media, DiVX, Scour and several others.

CHAPTER 8: POST-NAPSTER: WILL ONLINE SUBSCRIPTION PROSPER?

Online collaborations between the major record companies for online subscription services such as MusicNet and Duet make it easier to understand why they were so keen to close Napster down. But there are serious doubts whether the current attempts of the major record labels to prosper online will succeed. Concern centers mainly on the pricing and variety of offerings to an online audience psychologically accustomed to getting music online for free.

CHAPTER 9: NAPSTER, FILE SHARING AND PEER-TO-PEER – THE IMPACT ON THE WIDER BUSINESS WORLD

This chapter looks at how the success of Napster relates to the wider debate about the potential of peer-to-peer networking. The problem with any new development or trend is that people start to define the trend in terms of a buzzword or phrase. Pretty soon they start applying it incorrectly to too many things and, worse, the wrong things. This chapter defines what peer-to-peer really means and looks at some of the major operating systems upon which file sharing businesses could possibly be built in the future.

CHAPTER 10: NEWCOMERS AND OLD STAGERS

Such is the proliferation of peer-to-peer projects popping up all over the place that to pick out a few examples is very difficult indeed. But this chapter looks at three very different types of startup (Mojo Nation, Groove Networks and Living Systems), none of which existed five years ago. It also looks at the work done by three of what I have called old stagers (Microsoft, Intel and Sun Microsystems), although none of these three are particularly old companies by any traditional measures.

CHAPTER 11: IRRESISTIBLE FORCES AND IMMOVABLE OBJECTS

Here I look at two other types of companies that are making money out of peer-to-peer ways of doing business. The first group one could call the irresistible forces, examples of companies that are providing ways of using the essential elements of peer-to-peer not only through file sharing but also through, amongst other methods, distributed computing, distributed search engines and even mobile devices. The second group could be labeled immovable objects. These are the companies making a mint out of preventing the abuse of copyright, competing to develop watertight, unshakeable and immovable solutions to prevent its theft.

CHAPTER 12: CONCLUSION – NAPSTER, BUSINESS AND THE FUTURE

This chapter shows that although Shawn Fanning didn't invent file sharing or the wider concept of peer-to-peer networking, he inspired the development and debate over both. His achievement lies in helping to develop a "sharing" culture that is sweeping the world of business only five years on from the moment his uncle bought him his first computer. Even if Napster itself fades into obscurity, as it well might, the legacy of sharing has already started to reshape the business world.

It's always difficult to write about a subject matter that is continually evolving. The range of business developments either inspired by, or running alongside, Napster's development has become bewildering. I have tried to capture the main aspects of the business legacy of the Napster phenomenon but the process is moving on all the time. Apologies if I have omitted any worthy commercial contenders in the later chapters of this book.

One other thing to note: I have attempted to make it clear that many businesses and other organizations were developing ideas and themes on peer-to-peer networking even as Fanning and Napster were getting off the ground. I have tried to emphasize these different strands of thinking with "parallel lines" boxes, which highlight simultaneous developments elsewhere to those occurring with Napster.

Now some thank yous: my thanks to Mark Allin at Wiley-Capstone for coming to me with the suggestion that I write this book and his helpful suggestions on early drafts of chapters. Most of all, my thanks to my wife Melanie, who has put up with a lot during the writing of this book – thank you for your love and patience.

Trevor Merriden
St Albans
Hertfordshire
England
31 May 2001

CHAPTER 1

The Birth of the Napster Phenomenon

INTRODUCTION

THIS CHAPTER HIGHLIGHTS the extraordinary story of how Shawn Fanning came to write the source code for a file sharing program that the world now knows as Napster. It's a program that hasn't only changed the world of music; its impact has unleashed irresistible forces in all walks of life. It also has the potential to revolutionize the business world.

EARLY DAYS

The story of Napster starts in Brockton, Massachusetts in the early 1980s. In this small town lived the Fanning family. As a family of eight children, somehow shoehorned into a three-bedroom house, the Fannings endured many struggles. Both John Fanning and his elder sister Colleen experienced the tight squeeze along with their siblings.

One Saturday night, their elder brother threw a high school graduation party at the house and hired a band. It was only supposed to be a modest celebration for around a hundred friends but, perhaps in keeping with the wildfire word-of-mouth popularity of Napster nearly twenty years later, more than 3000 people turned up. The party was a mad house and Colleen met one of the band musicians – and ended up pregnant. The father, the son of one of the richest families in Massachusetts, quickly ducked out of his paternal responsibilities. Colleen, however, kept the baby and named it Shawn.

The early days of Shawn Fanning's life were pretty messy. Colleen went on to marry an ex-Marine but when they fell out, Shawn and his step-siblings went to live in a foster home for a year. During this turbulent period, John

Fanning kept an eye out for his nephew and tried to help him out whenever he could.

In 1996, when John bought Shawn his first computer and Internet connection, Shawn's life changed. Although he loved school sports, he rapidly stopped playing them to spend as much of his spare time learning about programming.

THE PHILOSOPHY OF SHARING

Shawn Fanning's life so far has been about the positive experiences of sharing information and experiences, and it is easy to see where the roots of his passion started. Almost everything that Fanning has learnt about computers came from one of two sources.

Firstly, during the summers in high school, Shawn worked at John's company, NetGames, as an intern, where he learned a lot about programming from kids who were studying computer science at Carnegie Mellon University. Secondly, he became a regular visitor to Internet chat rooms, where he picked up a lot of advice and information from more experienced programmers and developers: this latter source of advice was to become a major factor in helping him along. When visiting chat rooms, Fanning was obliged to give a user name; he chose his own nickname – Napster.

Fanning himself wanted to get onto the same course at Carnegie Mellon, but was turned down. Nevertheless, he won a place at Boston's Northeastern University and decided to major in computer science. Once there, however, Fanning found the set courses rather basic and looked around for extra challenges. He found one when he decided to go about creating various Windows based programs of his own. At around the same time, one of Fanning's roommates was obsessively interested in MP3s (see box below) and Internet music sites. Fanning was nowhere near as big a music fan, but couldn't ignore his roommate's complaints: the site was unreliable; many of the links often led nowhere; and indices were often out of date.

WHAT EXACTLY IS AN MP3?

One way for a computer to make noises is for it to decode music. This means that effectively, music is reduced to just a series of 0 and 1 bits. There's nothing intrinsically new about this – it's the way music compact discs work and the way Windows records and plays wave files, which is why your PC can play music CDs on a CD-ROM drive. Unfortunately, music files can be enormous. Wave files use about 10 megabytes of hard drive for each minute of music. So, if you wanted to send an album over the Internet using a bog standard 56K modem, it would take you nearly a day to do it.

This is why MP3 is so useful. It is the most popular of many ways to enclose audio so that the resulting file is squeezed to a tenth of the size of a wave file while still packing (near enough) the same sound quality. On faster Internet connections such as Digital Service Line (DSL), cable and T1, the download time is reduced to a couple of minutes or less.

When MP3 files are decoded back to the analog signals that create sound, there is almost no loss in sound quality between them and the original CD tracks. Why is this? Some sound is lost, but nothing too important, as the program usually strips out the quieter sounds on the recording or those below a certain frequency.

The MP part of the MP3 file comes from MPEG, a set of standards developed by the Motion Picture Experts Group for compressing and storing digital audio and video. The 3 in the name refers to MPEG Audio Layer 3, the part of MPEG that stores the audio.

A CLEAR VISION

Fanning decided to set about helping his friend. In his mind he had a vision of a system where people could share MP3s through the download of a piece of software. Fanning was pretty clear on his vision, and the piece of software is what we all know today as Napster. One friend who knew him at the time says, "Shawn did have a clear idea of what he wanted to do in the beginning. I don't know the exact moment when he first got the idea, but I'm pretty sure that he just woke up one morning in college and had an earth-shattering epiphany, something like 'Hey it would be neat if people could share their music with one another.'"

The importance of the community potential of the project to Fanning cannot be stressed enough. Fanning had learnt more in his life from talking to people than he had from traditional academic means. Put simply, he loved the idea that users would be able to chat to each other about, and share information about, their favorite types of music.

Although Fanning quickly became obsessed with what he was doing, the enactment of the dream was more tricky. He wrote a small design for his new search engine and then set about bringing his plans to life. He pursued two avenues: first of all he wrote the server software; he then started work on writing the software that the individual user would require. To do this, Fanning simply ordered a Windows programming book over the Internet to help him.

The system he visualized, a real-time system for locating the MP3 files of other Internet users, was quite unlike traditional search engines at that time. The old search engine model sends out what are known as "robots" to roam the Internet periodically, while the server updates itself every hour or more to remove sites that are down or no longer available. The database is dependent upon what a central computer finds by "crawling" the Internet. The problem with this is that the indices become outdated quickly. This is a significant problem when looking for MP3s because most of the files are to be found on people's home computers.

Fanning's dream was that if people were willing to share their files on a list that everyone could access, then that list could be updated each time a person logged on or off that computer. The computer would therefore always have an up-to-date list of the files people were willing to share. In contrast to the old search engine model, a search would be effectively powered by the user, who would choose the information they want listed. When the user left the application, their part of the list, that is to say the files they were willing to share, would automatically drop from the list.

Well the theory was great, but what about the practice of it all? Basically all Fanning had to do was to figure out a way to combine a multi-search function with a file sharing system and (to facilitate communication) instant mes-

HOW NAPSTER WORKS

Napster is, in some ways, something of a regression to the old days of the Internet. Mass usage of the Internet has meant that servers have to be used to house information. Napster, on the other hand, relies on communication between the personal computers of the members of the Napster community. Napster allows users to connect with each other to share MP3 files stored on their individual hard drives. The number of song files available at any given time depends on the number of song files that active users choose to share from their hard drives. Users need not share any or all of their files – they can choose to make what they want to make available. MP3 files do not pass through a centralized server. The transfer is made directly from computer to computer, known as "peer-to-peer." Napster cannot index files based on their content. Instead, such files can only be located and organized based on file names. The Napster service also provides location information allowing a computer to connect to the other user and transfer the file from its location. Other Napster functions include chat rooms, instant messaging, hot lists and message boards.

Napster makes it easy to search not only by the name of the artist or the song title, but by such important variables as bit rate, connection speed and ping rate. Why is this? Well, the bit rate refers to the sampling quality of the digital copy; in general, the higher the bit rate, the closer the recording is to the original. A bit rate of 128 or higher is, for most listeners, virtually equivalent to audio CD quality but the higher the bit rate, the larger the file. File transfers take forever if you are downloading to or uploading from someone who is using the equivalent of a hand-cranked modem. Napster allows people to restrict their music searches to computers that have high-speed connections. Listing your connection speed is voluntary and some people with fast connections may opt out because they do not want everyone to copy their music files.

saging. This would mean that he could bypass the red tape of legal and technical problems that kept people from sharing their music files. But he also had to find a way of combining the best features of existing programs; the instant messaging system of Internet Relay Chat, the file sharing functions of Microsoft

Windows and the advanced searching and filtering capabilities of various search engines.

THE MURKY WORLD OF w00w00

Suddenly, Fanning had a mission, but he needed some help from his friends in the chat room. One of these friends was Jordan Ritter, a teenage hacker. Fanning and Ritter met through their membership of an underground hacker group called w00w00 Security Development. This group is well known in the hacking fraternity as one of the most secretive organizations of hackers and technophiles in the world. Membership is strictly for fanatics only. Like any select club, exclusive membership brings with it certain comforts. Those who eventually become members feel relatively comfortable discussing their personal projects with each other, since it is generally understood that whatever is discussed in the group remains strictly confidential.

While Ritter is now recognized as a founding developer of Napster, he stresses that the concept was Fanning's alone, saying "Napster was essentially Shawn's first Windows program – meaning, kudos to him ... he wrote both the client and server software by himself." The concept was founded in the autumn of 1998 and at that stage there was no company or even any thought of one knocking around: "At that stage Napster really was just Shawn and a bunch of friends trying to help out. There were no venture capitalists, no uncles on the scene and no shady hangers-on" says Ritter, referring to the way Napster developed subsequently. According to Ritter, the days before Napster became well known were days of pure innocence, of friends trying to help out friends and share their knowledge. "Before Napster had taken its death grip on the Internet ... Napster was never a simple piece of software. Shawn Fanning would solicit his friends in 'w00w00' for help. I was one of those friends."

As Fanning got further along the road with what he called at the time his "MusicShare" application (his Napster nickname only came into common usage later), he started to run into some serious problems, and asked the group for help. Another of those who helped says, "I didn't know who Shawn Fanning was initially, but he was working on a really cool project and I didn't have any pressing personal projects on at the time, so I did what I could." Many of the other members of w00w00 felt the same way and began vying for his attention while Fanning was asking for help with increasing frequency as the project started to mushroom. Ritter says, "I myself was quite persistent, inferring what problems might exist and suggesting improvements without having access to the source code. As Shawn Fanning became more embroiled in the development of the project, he eventually asked me to take over the server development from him so that he could focus solely on the client. Soon, I took over both backend development and systems administration duties."

THE BATTLE AGAINST DOUBT ... AND TIME

There was another problem, quite aside from the technical issues. People kept telling him that users would be skeptical about whether other users would be willing to share files at all. One of the Fanning's chat room friends told him that the idea simply was not workable. "It's a selfish world and nobody wants to share," one older and more experienced hacker told him.

A lot of people would agree with that view, but every positive experience that Fanning had had up to that point told him that it was human nature to want to share experiences, thoughts and, yes, MP3s. Even selfish people, he realized, were up for sharing, as long as it did no harm to themselves. After all, people show each other their record collections, don't they?

That feeling drove him on ... and on and on. One college friend who knew Fanning well says that you have to understand this part of Shawn Fanning's character to truly understand Napster: "Shawn Fanning is an extremely determined character, young as he is. Part of the spirit behind Napster, in my opinion, was Shawn Fanning thinking this was a good idea and other people telling him it wouldn't work, simple as that. I believe he was driven more by the desire to prove to everyone that he was right than he was by any realization or recognition of a potential revolution." The intensity of this desire kept on getting Fanning into trouble in other areas of his life "I made the decision to leave school – I found I couldn't concentrate on developing the program and deal with my classes and life on campus. I was driven to figure out if I could make the program actually work."

What was emerging from Fanning's labors was what he wanted: a system for finding MP3s with chat rooms and instant messaging. He also added a "hot list" ability, which enabled people to see other's musical preferences by looking at the files they had chose to share. But the combination of different technologies needed testing and Fanning's big fear was that if he didn't act quickly others would do the job before him: "I figured that if I could make it work, others could too and someone else would take it from there."[1]

HERE COMES UNCLE JOHN

To prove his doubters wrong, Fanning decided to try out an early beta version of his software on 30 or so friends. He asked them all not to pass it on. His friends tried it, liked it and ... passed it on. Within a few days the software had been downloaded by around 3–4000 people. But many of the early users gave something invaluable back in return: they embraced Fanning's community vision and chose to give constructive feedback in sorting out bugs in the

---

PARALLEL LINES: SETI@HOME

In the same month that Shawn Fanning was trying to help people all over the world share music files, other projects in the world of business and research were beginning to develop as people came independently to the conclusion that sharing files, or even workloads, could be a good thing for everyone.

SETI@home is a scientific research project that is attempting to detect intelligent life on other planets. The radio data from the project is distributed over the Internet to individuals all over the world who use the individual disk space on their PCs to help in the search for extraterrestrial life. In May 1999, the project released downloadable software which allowed individuals all over the world to store broken down parts of all the data. Soon the project was overwhelmed by offers of help by enthusiastic volunteers, encouraged by the fact that processing of data was only to be carried out on each individuals' computer when that user had enough disk space to spare.

---

software. It was this sort of positive help that convinced Fanning that as well as designing the system, he should think about constructing it himself.

Shawn Fanning knew that he was onto something big and told his Uncle John. John Fanning quickly realized, as Shawn Fanning explained the project to him, that it had serious commercial potential. John Fanning had actually approved of his nephew's decision to drop out of college, and when he realized that his nephew was a potential pot of gold, he incorporated Napster into a company in May 1999 and went about raising money from investors.

There are different accounts of how this came about. John reportedly got 70% and Shawn Fanning got 30%, according to Business Week. According to one Napster insider, "I am told that this was done without Shawn Fanning's immediate knowledge or involvement. Newspapers have accurately reported the morally deplorable distribution of equity." While Shawn Fanning is still very much the public face of Napster, today he owns less than 10%, has no senior management position, isn't on the board and isn't involved in the company's business decisions. Instead, he still spends all of his time developing the company's software and acting as the company's public face.

Fanning Senior began to go around looking for Napster's first round of funding. The first person he spoke to was Yosi Amram, an old friend and Harvard MBA who had run product marketing for a small database company. Amram bought stock at 10 cents a share and before long Napster had enough

THE LEGAL SIDE: THE EARLY DAYS

One interesting sidenote: most people think of Napster as a bunch of kids who never even thought about the copyright issues that they were getting themselves involved in. The kids may not have, but certainly John Fanning, even at this stage was thinking about the legal issues. He hired the legal firm, Wison, Sonsini, Goodrich and Rosati, to discuss the potential issues involved and learned about many of the key legal precedents that would later form the basis of its lawsuit with the Recording Industry Association of America (RIAA). These talks gave Fanning Sr. the belief that he could carry on pushing the business forward and, more importantly, win any battle to come in court.

funding for another six months. Then Amran put in another $250,000 and brought in fellow tech entrepreneur Bill Bales, who invested $100,000 and became Napster's first hired employee as vice-president for business development. By October 1999, Napster had raised a $2 million second round of venture capital funding from the likes of Angel Investors founding partner Ron Conway and Excite@Home co-founder Joe Kraus.

50-HOUR STINTS, RED BULL AND PIZZA DELIVERIES – MADNESS IN SAN MATEO

At around this time Shawn and John Fanning, Ritter and another friend, Sean Parker, packed their bags and moved from Massachussets to Silicon Valley. San Mateo, in fact. The idea was that Uncle John would be better placed to go after the VC interests out on the West Coast. Meanwhile, the three youngsters, all involved in writing the beta version of Napster, were there to further develop the program. To start with, they were put up in a San Mateo hotel and are better remembered locally for their persistent attempts to sneak into bars while underage. Bales maxed out his credit card in the process and before long it was decided that they should move, along with newly hired employees, into a dingy, cramped office over a bank in downtown San Mateo.

One of the remarkable things about Fanning, said Ritter during this period, is that while he had a remarkably short attention span for detailed conversation, his determination and desire somehow carried him through to pound out software code for up to 50 hours at a time. His driving force was the quest for something that not only worked for the techies of this world, who could overcome its gremlins, but for something that worked for absolutely everyone, proving what a fine, wonderful, simple idea Napster was.

Fanning himself only dimly recalls the early fevered days of source code programming, but others have better memories. Ritter says, "In the beginning we were all driven by a kind of madness. Yes, I think that's the best description. I for one was simply overcome by the intoxicating madness of the thrill of the ride. I was pumping out code alongside the others, breaking for 30 minutes sometimes to have a white board discussion whichever one of us would get stuck, and then heading back to our desks, headphones up, feet on the table, keyboard in the lap, coding." 11pm would roll around, they'd order pizza, spaghetti and minestrone from Amici's and then go back to work. "It's so hard to explain any better, just that there was no life other than Napster that could exist. It was an addiction", says Ritter.

Certainly, these feverish souls were not at all worried about the seed money drying up. "Most of the time," says another insider, "we didn't care about anything else other than Red Bull and the odd snack. We were almost always isolated from the investors, so that was never a concern." All they cared about was the technology and the revolution that they hoped to inspire. Ritter adds, "I was in a daze and there wasn't much that could hold my attention beyond what we were working on." As for caffeine, Shawn Fanning's uncle, somehow lined up Red Bull as the team's authorized drink. "It came in by the case load delivered to the door! Brilliant!" he adds.

In such a situation of total and utter obsession, there were times when the team didn't go home and shower for days at a time and spent the whole time in the same jeans and t-shirts, often sleeping under their own desks. With Shawn Fanning working 50-hour stints, coupled with 16 and 20-hour days from the others, the team would reach a certain target – and then suddenly go nuts. There was one night in particular, says the insider, when the team found itself able to get over a million files shared on a server: "Shawn Fanning would play some old school notorious B.I.G., Snoop Dogg, or Dr Dre and we'd all just start freaking out and doing some wacky shit. Those were some fun times."

UNCLE JOHN MAKES NEW FRIENDS

While Shawn Fanning and his friends were working and playing hard. John Fanning was out making new friends who could help him.

Eileen Richardson was an early investor in Napster and became its CEO in September 1999. Richardson had spent ten years in the world of venture capital and seemed like a good choice for the startup phase of the company. In May 2000, she described her time at Napster to Salon.com: "As with any startup, you experience your highest highs and your lowest lows – the whole range of emotions. This is no different. Maybe the highs are higher and the lows are lower, but it's still that rollercoaster and that's what makes it exciting and fun."

Rollercoaster is no exaggeration. Richardson's presence gave employees a boost but her relations with the record industry and its legal representatives were frosty at best. She reportedly failed to get on with one very important person in the record industry: Hilary Rosen, CEO of the Recording Industry Association of America (RIAA). The two, according to one report, had virtual yelling matches down the phone over copyright lawsuits threatened by the latter (more of this in Chapter 3).

By the end of May 2000, Richardson had been replaced by attorney-turned-CEO Hank Barry. Hank Barry came to Napster as a partner at Hummer Winblad Venture Partners. Prior to that, he was a corporate and securities partner at Wilson, Sonsini, Goodrich and Rosati. He had over 15 years experience working with media and technology companies and had been counsel to Looksmart, Liquid Audio, Homegrocer.com and Viant. As a young man, Barry received a law degree in 1983 from Stanford, where he was also managing editor of the Stanford Law Review. All of this made a big impression on John Fanning. In Fanning's eyes, signs of his suitability for Napster can be found in the fact that he wrote award-winning papers in copyright law. Napster would clearly need such skills – and quickly.

"DO YOU HAVE ANY F**KING CLUE
WHAT WE'VE GOT HERE?"

Meanwhile, Shawn and the others had become so obsessed with the development of the project that they rarely got time to use their own creation. Another Napster employee says, "You know, I personally rarely used Napster. It's unfortunate on so many levels, not having time to enjoy what you worked so hard to create. But once in a while, I'd boot it up and search for rare material, like live Radiohead performances. What I'd get back would just boggle my mind – literally just make me sit there in silence and stare at my screen like an idiot. The realization hit me like a ton of bricks – I would just be obliterated. I'd download some esoteric live UK performance and listen to it several times, all the while screaming over my shoulder to the others "Jesus Christ, man, do you have any f**king clue what we've got here?" over and over. Then I'd snap out of it, look out of our San Mateo office window at the Bay, sigh, and get back to work."

When a beta version of Napster was named "Download of the Week," the company's Web site received over 300,000 hits. And once it became clear that Napster was spreading like wildfire across first American college campuses and then across the world, it's creators seemed bemused by the extent of its success. One says, "We knew it would be popular, but to be honest, I never really had any idea of the magnitude of impact the system would have and frankly, I don't see how anyone could. Who on earth would have figured those adoption rates? We didn't have to market the product, no advertising, no nothing. Who could have predicted that? Shawn Fanning always knew it would be big and I believed him, but I'm fairly sure even his own expectations were blown away very early on."

It would be hard not to be blown by the forces of peer-to-peer networking that Napster had unleashed. As the next chapter shows, the word about Napster spread more rapidly than anyone could possibly have imagined ...

NOTES

1   In a testimony to before the US senate judiciary committee in October, 2000.

CHAPTER 2

Why Napster Spread Like Wildfire

INTRODUCTION

THE FORCE THAT DROVE Shawn Fanning was the passionate belief that people wanted to share music and opinions *en masse* via the Internet. This was a pretty cool idea but many people, including several of his friends, doubted that enough people would want to share their record collections with complete strangers on the other side of the world. In the end, the friends were all very, very wrong and Fanning was very, very right.

THE WONDERFUL WORLD OF WORD OF MOUTH

You can understand the mentality of the skeptics. You can understand their logic. It's difficult to see how Shawn Fanning and a few of his techie friends swapping MP3s was going to amount to much more than fatter record collections for the few involved.

Welcome to the wonderful world of the word of mouth. Imagine Shawn Fanning and nine friends have a hundred MP3s each. Even when half of them are logged onto Napster, that's only 500 MP3s to choose from. And because Fanning's friends probably have similar musical tastes, there may be only 250 unique MP3s to choose from for any one user. You're probably better off going to a secondhand record store.

Because of this, some early users probably did become disenchanted with Napster's potential. But even if half the people logged off and never used Napster software again, as long as the other half sent the software to a single friend, they would have had the same number of MP3s and in all probability, some new and varied musical tastes. You can imagine how Napster suddenly became more interesting to both those who stayed and those who joined. If, in turn, they each told a friend, you suddenly have 20 people – and, potentially, a couple of thousand MP3s.

The number of MP3s grows. The variety of MP3s grows. The amount of time each user spends on the system uploading MP3s from other users' hard drives grows. The number of people each user tells about this impressive collection of free music grows. The number of people logging on to Napster grows … and so on and so on. This is the true power of peer-to-peer networking. Success breeds word of mouth; word of mouth breeds interest; interest makes further success a self-fulfilling prophecy.

So it was with Napster. A company that spent nothing on marketing and advertising spread like wildfire around the world through the sheer power of word of mouth. Even so, it helps if someone gives the product a helping hand with a bit of free publicity. It duly came with a feature on Napster on the Web site Download.com in the autumn of 1999, and the snowball grew in size from that point onwards. By October 2000, the Napster community numbered an estimated 32 million. The site at that time was growing by one million users

---

HOW MANY PEOPLE USED NAPSTER?

The truth is that nobody really knows. Because Napster has a central server, it has been possible for insiders to make some guesstimates, but the rest amounts to making up a number bigger than the one quoted before. There are some statistics from more reliable researchers. For example, Media Metrix, the international research agency, found the application on almost 10% of American computers connected to the Internet.

Yet it is inevitably the case that the bigger something gets, the harder it becomes to measure. By February 2001, just before Napster was shut down, another estimate put the number of Napster users at around 58 million. It could have been several million less or a hundred million more but what is important is that up until that time the number was huge – and seemingly always much bigger than the last time you asked.

per week, with 800,000 users logged on at times. The numbers grew even bigger thereafter and actually increased for a time after the court ruling that effectively shut down Napster in February 2001 (more in Chapter 4).

STUDENT REVOLUTION

Where do most self-respecting revolutions start? With the students, of course. In the US, Napster took a big early hold in the North-Eastern states such as Massachussetts and New York State, with over 40% of users coming from these states in the early days of its growth. It's no coincidence that a large proportion of college students are based in that part of the United States.

The early adopters of Napster were kids much like Fanning, Ritter and the others; young, usually in college and therefore with access to high bandwidth. Napster, of course, made one very powerful enemy – the Recording Industry Association of America, over the issue of copyright – but it also made colleges and universities distinctly nervous.

PANIC IN THE STAFF ROOM BARRACKS – "DON'T SHOOT THE MESSENGER"

It quickly became clear that Napster was spreading like wildfire across the college circuit. *Business Week* reported that at Oregon State University, Napster was occupying 10% of the school's Internet bandwidth by October 1999. Oregon State University's systems administrator, Chris White, noticed the trend early. The OSU decided to act quickly: "We noticed that there was a large amount of traffic that started at the beginning of the fall term. We did an investigation and found out that it was Napster." The OSU's decision to ban Napster came in the same month. It is important to point out that the decision was made as much on the grounds of cost and logistics as on the morals of copyright. The university was in danger of going well over budget for bandwidth and had to act. It estimated that with more students starting to use both Napster and to download streaming video, there was a danger that bandwidth would double every 90 days.

NAPSTER AND BANDWIDTH

Napster uses MP3 files, which don't take up too much space, but take up an awful lot of bandwidth. Why does Napster take up so much bandwidth? Well, for a start, Napster is not a site unto itself, but more of a network. There is a central server that coordinates all other computers, but these don't download off that central server. Rather, they download from each other. People end up downloading and uploading off each other with the data going both ways. The incoming pipe is already clogged up with all the downloading and if you add in the uploading, the pipes are even more clogged. Worse still, the way people used Napster would clog things up even more: some had Napster orgies where they searched for a bunch of songs they liked and downloaded them all at once. New users of Napster tended to do this more because of the novelty.

Meanwhile, at Florida State University, Napster was taking up 20–30% of bandwidth. Worse still, at the University of Illinois, the figure at one point was 75–80%. Colleges started to ban it and the record companies started to get serious with their threats of legal action against it.

With its popularity spreading as quickly as an Australian bush fire, hundreds of American universities decided to ban Napster in the fall of 1999 and the spring of 2000. At least a third took action, according to the technology research firm, the Gartner Group. Robert Labatt, principal analyst for Gartner's E-business Services Group says, "the reality is that the computer networks that have been set up at universities were built for academic services, not for music downloading." The pressure for universities to act was intense, he said at the time, "I would not want to be the university president who neglected to update the school policy regarding music downloads this year ... banning the online music service could prevent legal battles down the road." No doubt that the music companies or the Recording Industry Association of America would be more likely to take legal action against the school rather than the students.

New York University (NYU) acted early to ban Napster. Facing crippling network traffic that threatened to overwhelm the university's connection to the

Internet, officials slapped on a ban as early as February 2000. The university, in effect, had little choice. The program pushed the network's capacity to 98%, slowing access and threatening to crash it. And because the program effectively allows outside users to access the university's network, it was seen as presenting a security risk. Had they not acted, college officials argued, many network users and critical research programs would have been denied access to the Internet and the university would have suffered a denial of service attack. Certainly, once Napster was filtered out of the NYU system, the level of network traffic dropped immediately to 60% of capacity. Students were, predictably, furious. One NYU student said, "[They] made a decision without even talking to any students. I don't think that's an appropriate way to respond … there should have been some communication … at least warning students that Napster is a problem. If people are angry about this then they should speak up. [You're] paying for your bandwidth in your tuition."

Meanwhile, Hofstra University in New York, took a similar line to NYU. At around the beginning of 2000, Hofstra asked its Internet service provider to block traffic coming from Napster's software into its network, after noticing that the campus network was slowing considerably. Its Internet service provider, Applied Theory, started to warn Hofstra and many of its other clients – several of which were academic institutions – about the company. "Picture a large university with 20,000 students, many of them downloading this software," says Bob Riley, director of network services at Applied Theory, "More likely than not, they have set themselves up as servers. That can consume a lot of bandwidth."

IVY LEAGUE STRIKES A BLOW FOR STUDENTS

Some artists, noticeably the rock band Metallica and rap artist Dr Dre, were well known early opponents of Napster. The Los Angeles lawyer, Howard E. King, acting on their behalf, called on American universities to block access to Napster on their computers. MIT rejected the request, as did many others of the Ivy League type colleges, declaring, "As an educational institution providing its community of users with Internet access, we do not monitor or bar access to use of the Internet. This policy is consistent with MIT's educational mission and our deeply held values of academic freedom." MIT then covered its back-side by condemning copyright infringements. It promised to act if individual infringements were brought to their attention, but effectively did nothing. As Jeffrey I. Schiller, the network manager of information systems at MIT points out, "While usage patterns indicate that members of the community may be tuning in to Napster, the system has not become clogged. Maybe it's because our network connection to the Internet is large, or maybe our students aren't as Napster-happy."

Meanwhile, Harvard's Daniel Moriarty, Assistant Provost for Information Technology, took a similar approach to MIT: "The resources available through the Internet are an integral part of the academic and extra-curricular activities of students and faculty. Like other universities, Harvard provides network services that allow our community access to these resources. We do not monitor or regulate users' choices of sites to visit, nor their activities at given sites. A selective ban on access to particular sites based on the content of those sites would be inconsistent with the values of broad inquiry and the exploration of ideas that Harvard, like other universities, has traditionally sought to protect. We therefore decline your request." V. Lane Rawlins, President of Washington State University replied in similar vein: "The Internet is a resource that is an important part of the modern learning environment. We cannot presume that students are using the Internet for illegal purposes."

Nevertheless, the letters caused some institutions to choose their words carefully when speaking to students about Napster. Some of them, while not banning Napster, urged caution in downloading MP3 files. Boston College, for example, "strongly recommended that students, faculty and staff do not install or use Napster." It urged its students in particular to be aware of the hidden dangers of using Napster: "MP3 files are usually very large files, between 2 and 10 MB in size. Napster essentially turns every user's computer running the program into a server, causing a significant increase in network traffic and potentially slowing network access for users who require the network for their academic or administrative work. Furthermore, using Napster may leave a computer on the network more vulnerable to security breaches. By installing the Napster server on your computer you are providing anonymous access to your files to anyone on the Internet using the program. We believe this access

PARALLEL LINES: GNUTELLA

In the Spring of 2000, as students scrambled to download as many MP3s as their university bandwidths would allow, two men, Justin Frankel and Tom Pepper, were developing, in only fourteen days, what many now see as the best available alternative to Napster. Like Napster, Gnutella is all about file sharing. Unlike Napster, Gnutella had no central server at all – it was totally decentralized. Frankel and Pepper's bosses at AOL did not like the idea of file sharing one little bit and killed the project. Fortunately, other software developers picked up the project and ran with it. That they did paved the way to the development of ideas that have helped, in turn, to foster the commercial development of peer-to-peer networks (see Chapter 9 onwards).

may leave you vulnerable to the loss or damage of any files you store on your hard drive."

Of course, no one bothered to read these warnings, but it made the academics feel better about the dangers. Similarly, the University of Berkeley in California tried the "well it's up you, BUT" approach. Rather patronizingly, it warned, "Do not distribute or download copyright protected materials. Just because all your buddies are doing it doesn't mean it's OK. Penalties over piracy are stiff, a conviction in piracy can get you up to five years in prison with a fine up to \$250,000. If you get sued, you may need to pay damages of up to \$10,000 per title pirated." Enough to get any student running scared, surely.

Then there were those who put on a provisional ban only to lift it again, and those that upped their bandwidth capacity simply to keep their malcontent students happy. One university in Washington DC, for example, which blocked access to Napster in the spring of 2000, subsequently then went about improving its computer system to handle more Internet traffic and so restore Napster access.

In short, there were almost as many different reactions as there were institutions.

"MUSIC SHOULD BE FREE, MAN ..."

Of course, none of this had the slightest effect in deterring students hell bent on getting hold of free music. Students as a whole were completely unrepentant, believing that music should be free – take these examples from a report in the *New York Times*.[1] Stephen Goyne, a graduate of the University of California says that he uses Napster to fight back against record company profiteering: "Music should be made for the sake of music – it should be free." Mario Garcia from Berkeley says, "Come on – $15? Some people can't afford a CD." He adds that he would pay for the music if he had a job, but "what do they want more? For me to have a job and money, or stay in school?"

"If you're looking for someone to blame, blame the universities," says Amna Suharwardy, who attended summer classes at the University of California at Berkeley. The point that she and her fellow students make is of the "well, you left the door unlocked" variety: that to give students high-speed Internet connections that make it easy to download free music is like leaving a bottle of whiskey in front of an alcoholic. Another says, "People are going to use it. It's like putting $100 on the sidewalk – people are going to take it. They can make a criminal out of anybody."

The point about bandwidth in particular is a telling one. No one is surprised to learn that Napster's popularity among students has much to do with the fact that many of them are broke and certainly have no objection to getting their music for free. But the availability of bandwidth at college clinched its appeal. The average MP3 song file is more than 3 megabytes in size or more than 25 million bits. A cable or DSL modem is a fact of life at most colleges in the US and Napster probably would not be nearly as popular if college students did not have such easy access to 10 megabit (10 million bits per second) Ethernet connections in their dormitories.

WILDFIRE SPREADS TO THE 30-SOMETHINGS (AND BEYOND)

In October, 2000, Media Metrix, the international research agency, declared

NAPSTER ACROSS THE WORLD

The success of Napster in the US has been reflected by developments overseas. According to Canadian online researchers, In the Name of Cool, the number of Napster users in Canada increased by one million between May and November 2000. Towards the end of 2000 there were 2.8 million Napster users in Canada, compared with 1.8 million users six months earlier. The profile of Napster users in Canada has shifted a little over that time with the youth market now being joined by some older users as well, with 48% of users over 25 years of age, roughly the same as in the US. Moreover, the results of the survey indicate that awareness of Napster has nearly peaked in younger age groups. The rapid growth phase is now over and future growth will likely track the market penetration of high-speed Internet access. Furthermore, research firm NetRatings found Napster on slightly more than 6% of Internet-connected computers in the UK and Germany.

Napster the fastest-adopted piece of software in the history of computing. In just over a year of operation, Napster had amassed a file sharing community with 38 million registered accounts. These can't all be freeloading college students, so who else has been using it? The answer is – all of us. While 52% of Napster users are 25 years or under, 48% are 26 years old or over. Teens will, of course, always play a vital role in the development of online listenership. However, while teens will grow to 20 million online users in 2005, up from 13 million today, Napster usage by "silver surfers" has been growing even faster. Adults aged 35–49 are the fastest growing segment of the online population and will represent over 47 million online users in 2005, of which 9% will be aged 55 or over. This is where the Napster story becomes really interesting: although the early users were college students, its use has since spread to include a significant portion over 30 years of age.

BREAKING THE LAW (AND NOT FEELING BAD ABOUT IT)

Journalist Kelly Alexander explains all in the *New York Times*:[2] "I can attest that the people clinging to Napster are not just scruffy college kids; plenty of us are respectable mortgage-paying geezers in our 30s and up. We are over-aged teenagers for whom Napster is not just about freedom, but regression. The freedom to turn on a virtual radio that is always playing your favorite song, even if that song is Air Supply's 'Making Love Out Of Nothing At All.'"

Dubious musical tastes notwithstanding, Alexander describes a dinner party in which Napster was the celebrity guest: "Before I knew it, six mild-mannered adults were crowded around my desk, screaming out song requests like we were in a karaoke bar. 'It's like having your own juke box,' said a guest. Besides inspiring musical memories of youth gone by, Napster had the power to foster in grown-ups an adolescent compulsiveness. ... Among my friends, it opened up a reservoir of flashback teen angst. Like kids swapping baseball cards, we competitively traded downloads and bested each other with the most unusual versions of songs we could find."

What makes these older, otherwise law-abiding people want to break the law? The truth is that, psychologically, most people don't see themselves as law-breakers by downloading MP3s in their own home from their own computer. Yet the very same people would readily admit that anyone who makes their living as a writer or an artist deserves some respect for the copyright of their work courtesy of the laws on intellectual property. Yet somehow, while one half of one's brain is full of reasoned debate on the side of the artist, says Alexander, the other cruder part of the brain just can't help but love a song that you can dance, shout and scream to.

The sort of reasoning that Alexander captures so perfectly really sums up the emotions that anyone that has used Napster will know all about. The college circuit's early adopters saw their use of Napster as a combination of the "music should be free" ideology and a punishment exercise against greedy record companies, in the rather helpful world of the high bandwidth campus environment. For the older generation of users, however, motivations center much more around the pleasures of music downloaded with impunity and sheer nostalgia, the ultimate in white-collar victimless crime.

For many of the 30-plus generation, Napster is like listening to some sort of magical radio station full of your favorite songs. And taping off the radio is legal. And radio stations pay out royalties, don't they? The problem with this argument in relation to Napster is that here we all are running our millions of new "Radio-Me" stations and none of us are paying royalties. But when you're hunched over your keyboard looking for your favorite song that sort of thing is pretty easy to forget. There are no obvious penalties and the MP3 police are not going to come hammering down your door at 4 am.

The tacit breaking of the copyright laws also extends to the workplace in many cases. Ivan Cole, owner of Cole Systems, an e-business services company, runs an office in the US of nearly 100 employees, many of whom used Napster at work. "I learned about Napster from [my teenage daughter]," he says. "She showed me how she was downloading songs. I went out and got a CD burner. We started talking about it in the office. I strategically decided to open up the fire wall to allow anyone here to download Napster who wanted to." Napster as a recruitment tool? It's not nearly as far-fetched as you might think.

THE ADDICTIVE NATURE OF NAPSTER

Essentially, Napster made it easy for people to violate copyright laws, whether an individual user or a business wishing to keep its employees happy, without guilt or risk of capture. The popularity of Napster and its spread through the underground Internet had much to do with its simplicity. With an ordinary desktop computer and a modem, even the most computer illiterate of us can download recordings of virtually anything from the Beatles to Brahms, from the Prodigy to Puccini from any other Napster user without spending so much as a bean on either the software or the music. If you throw in a high-speed modem as well, then, well, the music world really does become your oyster.

It's not difficult to understand the addictive nature of Napster. People have no moral problem in observing laws whose only purpose seems to enrich corporate executive and lawyers ahead of the artists and performers. Many psychologists say that this attitude, when combined with Napster's simplicity, is a heady cocktail of factors that easily explain why so many people use it and why they will continue to try to use it even when the courts have declared such activity illegal. Peter Pollock, who teaches social psychology at UCLA says, "It is extremely easy for a user of Napster to say, 'the only people being hurt are the record companies, and they aren't paying the artists anyway.'"

Robert MacCoun is a distinguished law professor and social psychologist who teaches at the law school of the University of California, Berkeley. What follows from Napster, says MacCoun, is a classic situation in which breaking the law becomes acceptable because everyone is doing it anyway: "This is a kind of classic situation of what social psychologists call 'pluralistic ignorance'. The idea is that, often, social situations are ambiguous and we look to other people to help us define what's appropriate in a given situation. And we often infer from the fact that no one else is acting alarmed that there's nothing alarming going on. Everyone is agreeing tacitly not to ask the hard questions … it's a little reminiscent of the 1970s period when marijuana use became so prevalent that people acted as though it had been *de facto* legalized."

Even if people felt ashamed in some way about downloading Napster, they can more or less rest secure in their anonymity. If you download music from your bedroom under an assumed name, it doesn't feel like a crime. Even if there was no anonymity in your actions, it is hard to see how individual actions can cause so much harm. Kollock says, "The thought is that their one act makes no difference. The aggregate outcome is a different story. But individuals can credibly claim to themselves that they aren't impacting society."

Basically, we all live in our little world downloading our digital goods. And because these are digital goods, there's a feeling that you haven't deprived anyone of anything. Says Kollock, "I think we are rooted very, very much in the world of physicality, because that has been 99.999% of our history. Digital goods on a worldwide network is a very, very new environment."

WILDFIRE AND THE INDIE ARTISTS: SOME HAVE DOUBTS …

The spread of the use of Napster has naturally enough been particularly prevalent amongst music lovers. Some music lovers are also recording artists, but all recording artists are music lovers. Apart from Britney and her like, independent musicians and label owners have struggled to release music in a market that's absolutely dominated by the big time corporate labels. These artists have therefore tended to help spread the popularity of Napster, because it allows artists to independently distribute their music in an inexpensive manner, thereby removing pressure for them to work within the major label system.

The argument about helping out struggling artists through using Napster is a compelling one, but there is a downside to all this for the independent recording artist. Jenny Toomey, for example, is an independent musician and label owner in the United States. She says, "The downside to all this is a loss of control. There's a saying in the Internet community that goes, 'If you can hear it, you can copy it.' While this has been true since the advent of tape recorders, high quality digital copies are something new ... there is a sort of karmic payback to the major labels that have artificially inflated the cost of CDs. Sometimes it is seen as a backlash to commercial radio's bottom-line programming. I understand these arguments." But as an indie musician, who has already tallied up more than $10,000 in expenses against her unfinished solo album, she can't help but worry about future lost sales: "Now I worry that someone with an advance copy might offer the entire album via Napster before it's for sale. It is becoming increasingly clear that selling download tracks in the Napster environment is like trying to sell 50 cent beer next to a table that's giving it away. Worse still, the great majority of independent rock releases are sold to college age consumers – the very people who are consistently trading files."

... BUT MOST THINK IT'S GREAT

Other independent artists beg to differ. Steven Wendell Isaacs spoke up in favor of Napster in court when the RIAA started to pursue them. In his testimony he said,[3] "I believe that Napster is a powerful promotional tool for the many artists and bands that want to reach a large number of listeners but have not been able to get, or have been disappointed by, the support provided by large recording labels." A former MTV Video Jockey (VJ), Wendell formed a band Skycycle in the mid-1990s and was offered a recording contract by MCA records. When MCA delayed releasing the album until they reformatted it and re-recorded certain tracks, the band decided to post MP3s of their music to make it available to fans.

Shortly after, MCA threatened not to spend any money on promoting the band until the MP3s were taken down. "I was told that this order came from the highest regions of the corporate structure at MCA and Universal, which believed that any support for the MP3 format was unacceptable," says Wendell. "We took down our MP3s even though the band felt that the quickly increasing popularity of the Internet could make MP3 a viable and highly effective promotional tool. However, not only was there no extra money spent on the band's promotion, the album was never released." Wendell realized that under the terms of the contract, MCA had control over the recording and they decided to give it away online, the album becoming part of the Napster new artists' program in May 2000. The Napster MP3s resulted in the band getting fan mail from all over the world.

"We believe that the only way to generate interest for our music is to have people listen to it," says Wendell. "Considering what we, and hundreds of other bands, have been through with the antiquated business model of the major label, a program like Napster is a positive and powerful service for artists like Skycycle. Napster puts the power back into the hand of the artist and the listener. Taking Napster away from Skycycle will have a negative impact on the band's ability to reach out to, and create new, fans."

Nils Bernstein uses Napster, even though he happens to be Director of Publicity for Matador Records in New York. "There's a difference between theft and sharing music. We're against theft," he told the *Washington Post*,[4] but "kids [are] sharing music like they always have – and that's a good thing for the industry, that's a good thing for bands." Cliff Burnstein of Q Prime Management, which manages bands like Metallica and the Red Hot Chili Peppers, disagrees: "I don't believe there's the slightest chance that somebody's going to buy a track that they can get for free. 'Great, I just got that for free, now I'm going to pay for it?' It doesn't work that way."

THE JOY OF FINDING THOSE RARE RECORDS

Then there are the artists that benefit through producing rare, out-of-print records that can't be bought or found. Michael Lawrence, a recording artist and writer who, as a member of the band Sun60 from 1992 until 1996, has opened for the likes of Counting Crows and Paul Weller. The band was signed by Epic/Sony records until it withdrew support in the middle of one of Sun60's tours. He was let down by two other record labels in similar fashion. He points out that the reason why Napster is generally well-received by artists is that it "allows artists to reach their audience directly without having to rely on a recording label. Napster puts the power back in the hands of the artist by providing access to à worldwide community of millions who are eager and willing to explore new music. I wish Napster had been around back when the record labels failed me." In the meantime, years after Sun60 ceased to exist, Lawrence has discovered that Sun60 enthusiasts are trading their music via Napster. Is he angered by this? "I not only approve of this trading. I am flattered by it," he says. "It is a deep compliment and source of pride to know that the music I wrote and performed is being kept alive."

This is not just an ego trip for ageing artists. For some it makes a difference to their livelihoods. Lawrence W. Railey (also know as DJ Xealot) mixes techno, trance and dance songs. Before Napster, he says, only a few people were interested in his mixes. He posted some tracks on MP3.com and although some people paid to download his music, neither the income not the amount of traffic to the site was substantial. When he made his tracks available on Napster in November 1999, he also provided a link to his MP3.com site. Within two weeks of doing so, the traffic arriving at his sites improved by an estimated 50%, and revenue from the sales of his tracks picked up as fans flooded to his site. "I started receiving e-mails informing me that my music was being played in dance clubs, university radio stations and Webcasts worldwide. I have also received solicitations from various independent labels."

John Barlow co-wrote songs with the Grateful Dead for nearly 25 years. He says, "There is a significant group of musicians ... such as the Grateful Dead, who allow, and in some cases encourage, their fans to make recordings of their live performances. These musicians have discovered, as the Grateful Dead did, that the best way to make money from music is to give it away. While scarcity may increase the value of physical goods, in the information economy there is an equally strong relationship between familiarity and value. If your work is good, allowing what you've done to self-replicate freely increases demand for what you haven't done. Napster users are engaged in the online equivalent of tape recording. The free trading of music has fostered the careers of many bands and helped build their fan base."

So here we are back at the beginning of this chapter– the power of the critical mass. The bigger Napster grows, the wider the selection of music. The bigger the selection of music, the more users from all walks of life who are attracted to it and the more independent artists love it. Erik Gilbert is the VP of 75 Ark Entertainment, a recording company focused primarily on releasing hip-hop, DJ culture and turntablism products. 75 Ark made some artists' recordings available to Napster users for sharing because of its power as a marketing tool. Says Gilbert, "Napster allows the number of MP3s made available to grow exponentially. Every Napster user that downloads our artists' music becomes another source for that music. The trading of the bands' music by Napster users will help spread the word about the artists' music and is sure to increase the artists' fan base. Based on my experience in the music industry and marketing and promotion, it is clear that the inclusion of 75 Ark files in Napster's New Artist Program will drive more viewers to the artists' Web site, drive the artists' fans to purchase more music from the Web site and other retailers, and drive the artists' fans to attend live performances."

NAPSTER DISCOVERS ITS ENEMIES

Napster was a triumph of peer-to-peer networking. The implications of its staggering success have made people all over the world, including many in business sit up and take notice of the power of the critical mass. In the meantime, however, Napster made some very powerful enemies over its disrespect for copyright issues. Around the next corner, a combination of powerful record company executives and big name artists were getting ready to perform a mugging…

NOTES

1   "Backlash: a Binge on Music at State U" by Matt Richtel, *New York Times*, July 9, 2000

2   "The Day my Free Computer Music Died" by Kelly Alexander, *New York Times*, February 18, 2001

3   On 26 July, 2000, in San Francisco, CA.

4   "Napster shares files, raises ire" by Mike Musgrove, Robert Thomason, April 7, 2000.

CHAPTER 3

Big Boys Get Angry

INTRODUCTION

FROM THE EARLY DAYS of Napster, the five major record companies, both in-dividually and collectively, through the Recording Industry Association of America (RIAA), alongside big name artists such as Metallica, Dr Dre and The Corrs, grew in their hostility to what they saw as Napster's attack on their copyright. The frenzied popularity of Napster was a matter for deep alarm. This was a battle they couldn't afford to lose.

WHAT IS EVERYONE GETTING SO UPSET ABOUT?

> *"Information doesn't want to be free; only the transmission of infor-mation wants to be free. Information, like culture, is the result of a labor and devotion, investment and risk; it has a value. And nothing will lead to a more deafening cultural silence than ignoring that value and celebrating ... [companies like] Napster running amok."*
>
> Edward Rothstein, *New York Times*

It is difficult to put into words the apoplectic rage of large record companies over Napster: a combination of fear and indignation at the phenomenal growth of something of its kind, combined with desperate self-preservation. How could something which had no marketing budget which had spread by word of mouth grow so quickly and threaten to destabilize not only the record giants, but challenge the meaning of copyright in any area of business?

The fury of the recording industry was summed up brilliantly by Richard Parsons, co-chief operating officer of AOL Time Warner, speaking at a forum[1] in the middle of last year: "The defenders of Napster hide the reality of what they're doing – ripping off artists – behind the fig leaf of third-party neutrality. They claim they're merely acting as a matchmaker among Web music fans who want to exchange digital music files already in their possession. That's a little like a hijacker claiming he's doing nothing more than act as an intermediary in the transfer of property from one owner to another."

Napster was not only a hijacker, but a complete hypocrite in its attitude to copyright, he said: "Go to the 'Terms of Use' section at its Web site and this is what you'll read, quote, 'this Web site or any portion of this Web site may not be reproduced, duplicated, copied, sold, resold, or otherwise exploited for any commercial purpose that is not expressly permitted by Napster.'"

So there. If there was no law to protect Warner and its peers from Napster, argued Parsons, then who would protect Napster, or anyone else for that matter? "There's a passage in Robert Bolt's play about Sir Thomas Moore – 'A Man For All Seasons' – that sums it up concisely," he said. "Encouraged by his son-in-law to use the prerogatives of his office as Lord Chancellor of England to hunt out evildoers and heretics as ruthlessly as he can, Moore refuses. 'And when I'd cut down all the trees in England,' Moore asks, 'and given the devil no place to hide, where would I hide when the devil came after me?'"

Dramatic stuff from a clearly annoyed executive. Parsons and others wasted no time at all in cutting down as many trees as ruthlessly as possible in their pursuit of Napster. Parsons' experience as a lawyer told him that sooner rather than later the legislatures and courts were going to have to speak forcefully and definitively on the Napster issue: "Ripping off music is the same crime wherever it occurs, whether in a retail store or on a PC ... It's not just the legal ramifications of this assault on intellectual-property rights that convinces me a system which destroys a person's claim on his or her own work isn't going to stand. It's also the cold, hard facts of economic experience and common sense."

On one level, he argued, it seemed like child's play to go out and become a digital pirate, totally disregarding the issue of digital rights management – that is, who gets paid and who acts as the toll keeper every time the copyright is used. However, the long-term reality was somewhat different: "As soon as you face the grown-up question of starting a real business – a business that can sustain itself and grow in the legitimate marketplace and not merely survive furtively in the shadows – you have to deal with the fundamental issue of copyrights."

There were many in the industry who felt the same way as Parsons ...

THE MALCONTENTS

If you line up the five global record companies (Universal, Sony, Bertelsmann, EMI and Warner Music), you face five absolutely massive beasts with huge corporate clout. Set against Napster, effectively you have five Godzillas rounding on Bambi. Each had their own reasons for feeling disturbed by the success of Napster – and each had their own thoughts about possible ways out, some more constructive than others.

Vivendi Universal

Universal is perhaps better known as a film studio but the music side of the business came into its own in the latter part of the twentieth century. Its acquisition of PolyGram in 1998 established the Universal Music Group as the world's largest music company. In June 2000, Seagram announced a strategic business combination with France's Vivendi and Canal+, in what its architects saw as Universal's evolution into a fully integrated global leader in media communications and entertainment.

Today, UMG, a subsidiary of Vivendi Universal, has wholly-owned record operations or licensees in 63 countries around the world. It owns the most extensive catalog of music in the industry. Its businesses also include Universal Music Publishing Group, one of the industry's largest global music publishing operations. Universal Music Group consists of record labels too numerous to mention here but some of the better known ones include A&M, Decca, Deutsche Grammophon, Motown, Philips and Polydor, as well as a multitude of record labels owned or distributed by its record company subsidiaries around the world.

The impact of the Universal Music Group on today's industry cannot be underestimated. For the year 2000, according to SoundScan as tracked by "Billboard," it was the market-share leader for the top five categories: cur-

MORE ABOUT ... UNIVERSAL MUSIC GROUP

Universal Music Group is a small corner of the Universal/Vivendi media and entertainment empire, but is nevertheless absolutely huge in terms of the record industry. UMG's entertainment roots can be traced back nearly a century to 1912, when Carl Laemmle, an immigrant from Bavaria, founded the Chicago based Universal Film Manufacturing Company. Three years later, Laemmle moved his company to LA. He went on to produce a steady stream of silent movies, including Western comedies and action adventures. Universal Pictures grew into a fully-fledged movie studio and a leader in motion picture production and distribution.

Meanwhile, the Music Corporation of America (MCA), founded by Jules Stein in 1924, had been developing as a Chicago-based agency that booked bands into clubs and dance halls. The offerings of MCA were broadened by Lew Wasserman, who built MCA from a leading talent agency into an entertainment powerhouse. MCA and Universal started working together and then officially merged in 1962. With television and motion picture production firmly established in the early 1960s, the succeeding years comprised a period of growth and diversification for MCA/Universal, with the company expanding its interests into music. In 1991, Matsushita Electrical Industrial acquired MCA. Four years later, in 1995, a majority stake in the company was sold on to the Seagram Company. A year later, MCA was renamed Universal Studios, reclaiming its heritage as one of the industry's oldest and most prestigious movie studios.

rent and overall albums sales, singles, rhythm and blues, and country albums. UMG also held the No. 1 position on the "Billboard" Top 200 chart for a total of 21 weeks in 2000 with Eminem, Nelly, NOW 4, Limp Bizkit, LL Cool J, Ja Rule and Jay-Z. Among UMG's top-selling US titles were controversial American rapper Eminem's "The Marshall Mathers LP", Dr. Dre's "2001," Limp Bizkit's "Chocolate Starfish" and "The Hot Dog Flavored Water and Significant Others" and Shaggy's "Hotshot."

Universal has shown no reluctance at all to go after those that it has seen as pirates. In November 2000, the popular site MP3.com agreed to pay more than $53 million in damages to UMG. The previous April, a US judge had ruled that the site had violated copyright laws by creating a database of more than 80,000 albums. MP3.com settled with the other four record companies involved in the case, with Universal alone in holding out for more. "Universal Music pursued this case to send a strong message that copyrights will be protected and that copyright owners and artists need to be properly compensated for use of their work," said Zach Horowitz, president and chief operating officer at UMG at the time of the judgment. "Although we believe our proof at trial would have led to a greater damage award, we are satisfied with the award. It was never our intent to put MP3.com out of business with a judgment so large that it would threaten their viability as a company. We support the development of legitimate music businesses on the Internet."

The Universal artist Dr. Dre had gone on the record as criticizing Napster and pressured other record labels to do the same. They needed no encouragement.

Sony

Like Universal, the attitude of Sony Music to copyright infringements has been unrelentingly hostile. First of all they went after MP3.com with a copyright infringement suit. The resulting settlement allowed the online music site to use the Japanese record label's music as part of its internet-based service with MP3.com agreeing to pay Sony roughly $20 million in damages. The deal was the fourth in the series (described above) in which MP3.com settled with Time Warner Music Group (now part of AOL Time Warner), Bertelsmanns' AG music arm BMG, and EMI Group.

Sony has also been very aggressive in its pursuit of Napster. In 2000, the appropriately named Steve Heckler, senior vice-president of Sony Pictures Entertainment made a dramatic, almost Churchillian statement on the matter: "The [music] industry will take whatever steps it needs to protect itself and protect its revenue streams. It will not lose that revenue stream no matter what. Sony is going to take aggressive steps to stop this. We will develop technology

MORE ABOUT ... SONY

Sony's interests in music are based around the history of Columbia, the company that it bought into. Columbia traces its origins right back to the late 1880s, to the Columbia Graphophone Company of Bridgeport, Connecticut and the experiments of scientist Charles Sumner Tainter and his engineer colleague Chichester A. Bell, a cousin of Alexander Graham Bell. In place of the tinfoil phonograph of a decade earlier, the two men substituted cardboard coated with wax, on which a recording stylus traced sound patterns according to vibrations caused by impulses of sound projected onto it. By 1889, their new machine, the Graphophone was ready. Today, Gramophone is perhaps the more familiar word. In 1948, the company introduced the $33\frac{1}{3}$ rpm LP (or long-playing record), which revolutionized the industry. Earlier, Columbia had been bought by William Paley's Columbia Broadcasting System (CBS). And in 1968, CBS entered its first joint venture with Sony Corporation, which twenty years later was to result in the latter acquiring the former, known today as Sony Music Entertainment. In 1994, Sony Music Entertainment was reorganized into four label groups: Epic Records Group, Columbia Records Group, Relativity Entertainment Group and Sony Classical.

that transcends the individual user," he said. "We will firewall Napster at source – we will block it at your cable company, we will block it at your phone company, we will block it at your [Internet service provider]. We will firewall it at your PC. These strategies are being aggressively pursued because there is simply too much at stake."

Perhaps more so than any of the other big five players, Sony has a technological expertise that stood it in good stead in moving quickly in the battle over digital rights. Even so, Sony is by no means the wronged party on all occasions when it comes to copyright issues. Last year a group representing thousands of record stores said it was suing Sony Music Entertainment for allegedly forcing retailers to sell CDs that drive consumers to Sony's online stores. The threat of litigation highlights the dilemmas for companies like Sony. On the one hand, record companies were trying to protect their property from online pirates, but at the same time, they began to look at the possibility of selling their product directly to the online consumer. Such a balancing act didn't stop them from going after Napster big time.

Warner Music Group

The attitude of AOL Time Warner towards Napster has been one of unremitting hostility. The ability of the organization to respond has been partly impaired by the ongoing mega-merger between AOL and Time Warner, following on from the merger between Time and Warner. Richard Parsons, co-chief operating officer at AOL Time Warner, noted that a combination of the Internet and software that made it easy to locate and select files from other computers – and to do so anonymously – undermined traditional understanding of copyright. He went on, "Dorothy Parker once said that, though the best things in life may be free, the really enjoyable things are either illegal, immoral or fattening. Unlike a lot of activities, swapping MP3 music files on the Web isn't fattening. But since it involves a clear violation of the copyright laws and ignores the rights of artists to the fruits of their talent and labor, it is immoral and illegal."

"Think about it a moment," he continued, "On the human level, what musicians or writers or filmmakers are going to invest years of hard work and talent in producing work that will bring them zero financial return? On the corporate level, who's going to invest in nurturing and developing talent, building studios for films, music and programming, and supporting an enormously expensive creative infrastructure with the guarantee everything they produce will be instantly and universally pirated? Without a legal framework to control the distribution of digital files – a framework that acknowledges and enforces copyright protection – it's hard to imagine anyone but non-profits or proselytizing organizations bothering to get involved. Personally, I find it impossible to believe that the music industry is going to end up under the direction of the Salvation Army. That's not because I don't respect the Salvation Army. I do."

Even so there is a general recognition that the major labels, Warner included, have not really got their act together properly in any big way. Says Parsons, "The record companies must compete online. The major labels have been asleep at the wheel. We've been hesitant to change from older business

MORE ABOUT ... WARNER MUSIC GROUP

Here are some facts that will make you realize just how enormous Warner Music Group really is: it operates through companies in over 65 countries and its labels include Warner, Elektra and Atlantic. Warner/Chappell is its worldwide music publishing company and has over one million songs in its catalog. Approximately 38% of its revenue comes from US recordings while more than 53% of its total revenue is generated outside the US. Warner's part in the stranglehold of music distribution is clear: the five major music companies have approximately 80% of the recorded music market between them, up from around 60% ten years ago. Warner Music has an approximate 12% market share.

Six countries – the US, Germany, the UK, France, Japan, and Brazil – represent about 75% of the world's record market and, for Time Warner, the US is the largest market. The company ended the year 2000 third out of fifth in market share in the US, just behind BMG. Historically, overseas AOL Time Warner has been weaker than the other majors, all of whom started as foreign companies, but the revenue figures suggest that the company is catching up overseas. Warner's most famous music artists include Madonna, Red Hot Chili Peppers, The Corrs, Eric Clapton and All Saints.

models. And consumers have made it absolutely clear they want to get music digitally."

Roger Ames, the chairman and chief executive of Warner Music Group, made many of the same points in a speech[2] at the beginning of 2001: "We do know that there's a huge demand for digital music. It will produce new revenue streams, it will expand the consumer market, and most importantly, it will expand consumer choice by making all music available all the time. It will also allow for one-to-one marketing to consumers, not something we've had in the past ... We're only just learning how to use the power of the Internet to market, to promote and distribute music in new ways. At the same time, we have to deal with piracy. Piracy is not new to this business, but now it is in a new digital form."

EMI Music

EMI has been less harsh in its anti-Napster rhetoric. While it joined the other big five record companies in challenging Napster over copyright issues, it preferred instead to focus its energies on the possibilities of peer-to-peer networking. EMI chairman, Eric Nicoli, says that new media developments represent considerable growth opportunities for the music industry which, he believes, outweigh the potential risks of piracy: "We are remodeling our business in order to maximize the opportunities and benefits of the new environment. This involves digitizing 100% of our global content, developing business models for digital downloading and exploring important new marketing and promotion opportunities."

What does this mean exactly? Well, EMI has been involved in a number of alliances in new media activities ranging from Internet sites to live concert Webcasting and Internet radio channels. In most cases, an equity stake was taken as part of the agreement. Also, EMI, in conjunction with a number of other companies including representatives of the music and consumer electronics industries, has been supporting the Secure Digital Music Initiative. And in an aggressive move to sell digital downloads in 2000, EMI made an extensive archive of its music catalog available online, announcing that 200

MORE ABOUT ... EMI

EMI is perhaps most famous as the label that gave the world the Beatles but it's history goes way back to the nineteenth century. For over 100 years, it has been one of the world's leading music companies and today, the EMI Group operates directly in 45 countries, with licensees and distribution agreements in a further 26. EMI releases more than 1000 albums every year.

EMI Recorded Music's labels include EMI, Virgin, Capitol, Parlophone and Chrysalis. The group is also one of the world's leading music publishers, controlling over a million copyrights spanning the whole musical spectrum. Artists signed to the group include Janet Jackson, Lenny Kravitz, Robbie Williams, Diane Warren, Sting and Puff Daddy.

---

singles and 100 full-length albums from its back catalog would go on sale, the idea being that EMI will continue to release more albums until its entire library is available.

Bertelsmann

Notable by its absence from the Napster debate in the first half of 2000 was Bertelsmann. While maintaining the necessary public hostility to Napster that the other record labels expected, it soon became clear that its attitude was different. Effectively, Andreas Schmidt was the man behind the change in attitude: the president and CEO of Bertelsmann eCommerce Group was former

---

BERTELSMANN MUSIC GROUP

The media and entertainment group may be relatively enlightened when it comes to peer-to-peer technologies but its roots go back very deep. In July 1835, the printer Carl Bertelsmann (1791–1850) founded C. Bertelsmann Verlag with its own book-printing plant in Gutersloh. 165 years later, the company is simply enormous. In the year 2000, Bertelsmann had revenues of DM 32.4 billion and over 75,000 employees. The company has operations in 58 countries. A quarter of its revenues come from books and a similar amount from BMG Entertainment (which includes music). It now makes more money from the US (about a third) than in its native Germany (about 30%), with a similar amount again being made from the rest of Europe. The company is over 70% owned by the Bertelsmann Foundation, with the rest owned by the Mohn family (21.4%) and the Zeit Foundation (7.5%).

BMG Entertainment may be about a quarter of the Bertelsmann empire but in itself it is huge. It has revenues of $4.7 billion and has 11,690 employees. Its core areas are record labels and music publishing and it sells over half of what it does into the United States. BMG Entertainment is the number one distributor of singles in the United States and number two distributor of current albums in the United States. In addition its Sonopress operation is the largest CD-ROM and third-largest CD manufacturer worldwide.

---

head of AOL Europe and, on taking over his first acquisitions, CDnow and Barnesandnoble.com, Schmidt could see which way the wind was blowing. AOL had been making noises about creating its own music subscription service using Time Warner's Warner Music Division. Other big music players, like Universal Music Group and Sony Music Group, were developing their own subscription services as well. While the others huffed and puffed, Bertelsmann kept its own counsel, as we shall see in Chapter 6.

THE HENCHWOMAN – HILARY ROSEN AND THE RECORDING INDUSTRY ASSOCIATION OF AMERICA

While the big five each took their own individual stances on the Napster issue, they coordinated their efforts through the Recording Industry Association of America (RIAA). At the center of the record industry's drive to re-establish the rules of copyright has been Hilary Rosen. As the CEO of the RIAA, Rosen is the most visible spokesperson for the entire music industry and has had the unenviable task of addressing the growing tide of feeling against the record industry arising from the debate over Napster. Before Rosen arrived, the RIAA had been a sleepy trade organization that was neither a public entity or had any public profile. Rosen's arrival in the late 1990s coincided with the need for a far higher profile.

Few ordinary people shed tears over the copyright issues of large record companies and certainly, the RIAA has gained few fans among online communities over their stance against Napster. However, Rosen has never been the hostile arch foe of online music distribution portrayed by many on billboards and chat line forums all around the world. Chuck D, the founder of the rap group Public Enemy and a vocal critic of the major record labels and their attitude towards Napster, described Rosen as "a lioness protecting the asses of five cowards."

Lioness or not, Rosen has been keen to emphasize that it is in everybody's best interests that copyright agreements are respected: "It is better to work with the creative community than against it. … [The battle with Napster] has always been about sending a message to the technology and venture capital communities that consumers, creators and innovators will best flourish when

WHO IS HILARY ROSEN?

Hilary Rosen is the chief executive officer of the Recording Industry Association of America, the Washington-based trade group that represents the nation's largest record conglomerates, as well as many independent record companies. As the first woman to assume such a powerful position in the trade group, Rosen has led the association's attempts to bring on protection systems for music recordings in the digital age. She joined the RIAA after getting her start as a Washington lobbyist in the early 1980s. Her efforts have helped the music industry secure an amendment to the Copyright Act that provided special clauses for sound recordings. The group's members, which include the big five record companies – Warner Music Group, Sony Music, Universal Music Group, Bertelsmann Music Group and EMI Music – manufactured and distributed more than 90% of the $12 billion-worth of annual sales of records in the US in 2000.

copyright interests are secured. It has never been about peer-to-peer technology itself, which can be implemented legitimately."

In an interview with *Salon.com* magazine[3] last year, Rosen was adamant that legal action was a short-term imperative, but was realistic enough to admit that it was not the long-term solution for the record industry: "There is certainly a lot of intrigue in the notion of file sharing – for community reasons and for marketing reasons and for putting people with like-minded interests together. Clearly I understand all that. But those issues really should be divorced from the very unique and specific issue: does a company have a right to create a system that is so deliberately designed to take other people's work?"

But how can the likes of record companies win with so many mini-Napsters springing up all over the place? Certainly, the debate has forced people like Rosen to rethink. Rather than preside over a record industry trying to stop new innovations, Napster and the online distribution of music has caused the record industry to rethink its business models.

There's no question that the record industry has been slow getting to the online marketplace, but it's too simplistic to say that this is because of fear,

PARALLEL LINES: THE RISE OF DRM

Hilary Rosen was probably understating the case to say that the notion of file sharing was causing "intrigue." It was, in fact, causing palpitations among many content providers both inside and outside the record industry. On the same day that Rosen made her statement to *Salon* magazine, Intertrust, a digital rights management (DRM) solutions provider, was announcing a deal to provide DRM software to Compaq products for music distribution. This was just one of many deals that Intertrust unveiled in a period where companies were scrambling around frantically to address the issues of copyright infringement threatening to kill all of their businesses stone dead. The success of Napster's file sharing program was bad news for content providers but great news for the likes of Intertrust (more on this in Chapter 11).

although there is certainly some fear involved. It's more accurate to say that these are very complex transitions with a lot of interests and players involved and giant record companies have had problems adapting quickly enough to a wholly new situation.

Another of the arguments that justifies Napster's use is that it makes listeners go out and buy more CDs rather than less. The point, says Rosen is not whether CD sales are rising in spite of Napster (see box below), but that the owners of Napster are building a business on the backs of artists: "Cynics say the record industry doesn't like that model because it takes them out of the equation. But it's not true – artists like it when they have a record that's so successful that they get to stay home for a few months rather than go on tour. You are limiting the artists' choices. And secondly, a significant part of the meaning of the music is creating the demand for the work. And creating that demand for the music and the artist is very much a marketing and promotional function the record company does. The costs associated with that have to be absorbed somewhere."

DOES NAPSTER HELP RECORD SALES?

Derek Sivers is founder, president and CEO of CD Baby. Founded in February 1998, CD Baby is an online record store, selling and shipping CDs by independent artists only, worldwide. He says, "Because of the tremendous exposure and promotion the Napster system provides for artists that may otherwise remain unheard, the Napster system is substantially contributing to the sale of CDs on CD Baby. Because of Napster and other programs and systems like it, music is becoming a bigger part of many people's lives. Napster users have the ability to listen and sample all kinds of music easily and conveniently. This increases the possibility that those users will hear music that they may have otherwise missed. Based on my experience as a music retailer, it is clear that Napster, like anything that keeps the public interested in music, helps the music and recording industry as a whole, especially independent bands."

THE BIG ROCK STARS – LARS GETS ANGRY

When you're under pressure already, probably the last person you want turning up on your doorstep is Lars Ulrich. The Metallica drummer and a lawyer showed up at Napster's Silicon Valley headquarters in early 2000 with 13 boxes of computer printouts purported to contain the names of 335,435 Napster users who had swapped Metallica MP3 files. The documentation also identified 1.5 million MP3 files of 95 different Metallica songs that were supposed to have been available to download over a two-day span.

Metallica was not the only big name group to speak out against Napster, but somehow Ulrich has become known as a sort of figurehead in the pop industry against the phenomenal spread of Napster. Born in Denmark, Ulrich and his parents came to America in 1980. In 1981, as a teenager, Ulrich started a band named Metallica with his best friend James Hetfield. By 1983, they had released their first record and achieved a great level of success in the music business throughout the world.

Early in 2000, while completing work on a song for the movie *Mission Impossible 2*, Ulrich was startled to hear reports that a work-in-progress version

WHAT DO OTHER BIG-NAME ARTISTS THINK OF NAPSTER'S SYSTEM?

Here are just a few examples of what artists are saying:

"Many artists have spent their lives honing their craft and now some anonymous person in a little dark room with a computer somewhere is able to collate that lifetime's work and pass it around the world for free. It's just not on. Stealing is stealing regardless of what name you choose to call it."

Matt Johnson of The The

"I am excited about the opportunities presented by the Internet because it allows artists to communicate directly with fans. But the bottom line must always be respect and compensation for creative work. I am against Internet piracy and it is wrong for companies like Napster and others to promote stealing from artists online."

Elton John

"Artists, like anyone else, should be paid for their work."

Lou Reed

"Napster presents huge problems for the artists. It raises the questions – which is positive – of where and how artists are compensated. But I don't agree with the model they've set up. The artist should be the person who's ultimately in a position to decide when, where, and how something should be shared with whomever they choose to share it with."

Alanis Morissette, *Yahoo! Internet Life*, August 2000

was already being played on some US radio stations. He traced the source of this leak to Napster. Ulrich and Metallica learned that all of their previously recorded copyrighted songs were, via Napster, available for anyone around the world to download from the Internet as MP3s.

Says Ulrich, "We became the first artists to sue Napster, and have been quite vocal about it as well. We have many issues with Napster. First and foremost, Napster hijacked our music without asking." Napster, he says, never sought Metallica's permission, as their catalog of music simply became "available" as free downloads on the Napster system. "I don't have a problem with any artist voluntarily distributing his or her songs through any means the artist elects – at no cost to the consumer, if that's what the artist wants. But just like a carpenter who crafts a table gets to decide whether to keep it, sell it or give it away, shouldn't we have the same options? My band authored the music which is Napster's lifeblood. We should decide what happens to it, not Napster – a company with no rights in our recordings, which never invested a penny in Metallica's music or had anything to do with its creation. The choice has been taken away from us."

Let's look at the real costs of a band like Metallica. When Metallica makes an album it spends many months and many hundreds of thousands of dollars writing and recording. It typically employs a record producer, recording engineers, programmers, assistants and, occasionally, other musicians. It rents months at a time at recording studios and its record releases are supported by hundreds of record company employees and provide programming for numerous radio and television stations. Says Ulrich, "Add it all up and you have an industry with many jobs – a very few glamorous ones like ours – and a greater number of demanding ones covering all levels of the pay scale for wages which support families and contribute to our economy."

Metallica is fortunate that it makes a living from what it does. Ulrich's point is that artists are barely earning a decent wage and need every source of revenue available to scrape by, and the primary source of income for most songwriters is from the sale of records. Every time a Napster enthusiast downloads a song, it takes money from the pockets of the creative community, says Ulrich. If music is free for downloading, the music industry is not viable; jobs will be lost and the diverse voices of the artists will disappear. Says Ulrich, "The argument I hear a lot, that 'music should be free,' must then mean that musicians should work for free. Nobody else works for free. Why should musicians?"

Metallica claims not to be anti-technology. When the band made its first album, the majority of sales were in the vinyl record format. By the late 1980s, cassette sales accounted for over 50% of the market. Now, the compact disc dominates. Ulrich concedes, "If the next format is a form of digital downloading from the Internet with distribution and manufacturing savings passed on to the American consumer, then, of course, we will embrace that format too. But how can we embrace a new format and sell our music for a fair price when someone, with a few lines of code, and no investment costs, creative input or marketing expenses, simply gives it away?"

How does this square with the level playing field of the capitalist system? Says Ulrich, "In Napster's brave new world, what free market economy models support our ability to compete? The touted 'new paradigm' that the Internet gurus tell us we Luddites must adopt sounds to me like old-fashioned trafficking in stolen goods."

Certainly, a look at Napster's "terms of use" shows that Napster itself wants the benefit of copyright: "This web site or any portion of this web site may not be reproduced, duplicated, copied, sold, resold, or otherwise exploited for any commercial purpose that is not expressly permitted by Napster ... all Napster web site design, text, graphics, the selection and arrangement thereof, and all Napster software are Copyright 1999–00 Napster Inc. All rights reserved Napster Inc ... Napster, the logo and all other trademarks, service marks and trade names of Napster appearing on this web site are owned by Napster. Napster's trademarks, logos, service marks, and trade names may not be used in connection with any product or service that is not Napster's."

This rather begs the question, says Ulrich, that if Napster itself wants – and surely deserves – copyright and trademark protection, why should the creators of music and intellectual property be denied the same protection?

THE STORM APPROACHES

With an array of powerful forces lined up against it, it was inevitable that sooner rather than later the lawyers would get involved. The first shot in a long and bitter war came in the form of a letter that landed on the doormat of Napster headquarters in December 1999 ...

NOTES

1   Richard Parsons was speaking on "The Future of Music" on July 24, 2000 at the Jupiter Communications and Billboard Plug-In Forum.

2   Roger Ames was speaking at the AOL Time Warner Investor Day on January 30, 2001.

3   *Salon.com* magazine, May 1, 2000.

CHAPTER 4

The Battle Commences

INTRODUCTION – SHOTS ACROSS THE BOW

CONTRARY TO COMMON UNDERSTANDING, Napster was not just a bunch of free-wheeling techies with no comprehension of copyright laws. John Fanning, Shawn Fanning's uncle and chief business strategist at Napster, claimed to have personally read previous court rulings on the subject. So confident was he that Napster was in the right that he sent out an e-mail within the company suggesting that there was only a 10% chance that Napster could lose any threat to it from the major record labels.

Such a gung-ho attitude to their fate was reinforced by the recruitment of Eileen Richardson as CEO for the Napster startup phase. Richardson had little experience of running a business, but she was respected by venture capital firms. Earlier she had led an investment in Firefly, an Internet service that recommends music, which Microsoft liked enough to buy. Former Napster employees report that following the first contact between the RIAA and Napster in August 1999, negotiations between Hilary Rosen's team and Eileen Richardson quickly degenerated into hostile and destructive exchanges down the phone. One employee confirms that Richardson had animated phone calls with Frank Creighton, the head of the RIAA's anti-piracy group, and face-to-face meetings with Rosen that did not go at all well.

Former Napster staff say that Richardson was both combative and inexperienced in her handling of the situation. Others say that the discussions simply brought into focus a huge clash of cultures and monster egos. In spite of all this, venture capitalists and Napster employees say that there was a point at which a deal seemed more likely than not. *Business Week* reported that in late November, one former employee claimed to have met with an executive from a major record label who gave him the impression "that there was a deal

PARALLEL LINES: FLYCODE

At around the same time that Napster was first sued by the major record labels, the early Napster founders and investors, Bill Bales and Adrian Scott (see
Chapter 1), took the Napster file sharing ethos down a safer route. They announced the formation of a company known as AppleSoup. The idea was that
this was the next generation of peer-to-peer distribution and would allow content owners to distribute "anything digital" via the Internet while giving them a
way to control and monetize their intellectual property. The idea of Flycode
was to head strictly down the road of legality, working with, rather than against,
content providers in music, video and films. Even so, the startup was immediately threatened with legal action by Apple Computers on account of its original
name. The name was quickly changed to Flycode (see Chapter 7).

in hand." The talk, says the magazine, did not get very far, but the general idea
was to sell a minority stake in Napster to the company and allow Napster to
license a host of content from one label. That deal could then be used as lever-
age to approach another record label.

In the event, nothing came of the talks and in December 1999, the major
record labels sued Napster for copyright infringement.

THE CASE FOR THE PROSECUTION

At the center of all this activity was Hilary Rosen at the RIAA. The RIAA,
on behalf of its members, says it sued Napster because it launched a service
that enabled piracy of music on an unprecedented scale. Napster had built
a system, it said, that allowed users who log onto Napster's servers to obtain
infringing MP3 music files. The RIAA claimed that the overwhelming majority
of the MP3 files offered on Napster were infringing.

Just because Napster itself may not house the recordings, argued the
RIIA, did not mean Napster was not guilty of copyright infringement. Copyright law, it claimed, was clear: someone who materially contributes to infring-

ing activity, with knowledge of that activity, is liable for copyright infringement as if that person did the copying him or herself.

Surely Napster's copyright protection page clearly says it revokes the ability of users to access Napster if they breach copyright law. Isn't that enough? From the RIAA's perspective, these were just words. In fact, Napster's Web site had some rather provocative words on it. Napster touted itself as the "world's largest MP3 music library" that "ensures the availability of every song online." Not only did Napster know about copyright infringement, said the RIAA: it positively encouraged it.

The RIAA was adamant from the outset that its aim was not to stop the use of MP3 technology. The example it came to use in court was that of an ATM card. Keeping someone from trying to use your ATM card, for example, doesn't mean you are trying to stop the use of ATMs. As for MP3 technology, the RIAA stated that it only had a problem with the illegal uses of the format to distribute copyrighted recordings without the permission of the artist or record company.

The true issue arises, says the RIAA, when you consider that Napster and other file trading services are setting standards and expectations from consumers that labels and artists can't reasonably meet: it's not fair to create an

WHY NOT GO AFTER THOSE THAT USE NAPSTER RATHER THAN NAPSTER ITSELF?

MP3 is not to be confused in terms of legality with the ill-fated Napster. MP3 is, in itself, a legal format. Its uses include copying the CDs you own onto your computer and making recordable CD copies of those same recordings. Common downloading of MP3s isn't likely to get individuals into trouble, unless you make thousands of copies and start selling them on the black market of course. For the record companies, it makes far more sense economically to go after those who provide a platform for copying than to go after the individual users who would probably cost far more to prosecute than the record companies could get back in lost revenues. And the whole area of personal use MP3 files is far more dangerous legal territory for the record companies.

illegitimate service – and then force copyright holders to participate in it as a means to ensuring their future.

Did the RIAA want to put Napster out of business when it filed suits? Apparently not. A spokesman said, "No. We're only asking them to stop the unauthorized distribution of music. We want Napster to play by the same rules as everyone else, including the copyright laws honored by businesses offline and legitimate sites online that are licensed to download music." Not even the RIAA would claim that Napster would put their members out of business: "While the Napster case is incredibly important to the recording industry, the vast majority of the industry's product is still sold in bricks-and-mortar stores. That isn't going to change overnight." Which makes you wonder why they were so keen to go after Napster in the first place.

The key point, said the RIAA, is the difference between file copying and file sharing. There is a big difference between a consumer making a copy for a friend, and that same consumer making the file available on Napster where it can be freely downloaded by millions of people. You don't have to be a copyright lawyer to know that it is not "fair" to allow an individual to make copies of copyrighted music available to millions of anonymous strangers. The RIAA have a point here: this is file duplication on a massive scale. Sharing is when one person gives up something for another. With Napster, nobody is giving up anything because everybody gets to keep a copy.

Another frequently asked question is how is file trading different from recording from the radio? Taping a song from the radio for your personal use is nothing like file trading. Unlike radio, file trading allows you to search for specific songs and access them at will. Most importantly, says the RIAA, the harm that can be caused by file trading over the Internet is several orders of magnitude greater than the impact of off-air taping.

At the heart of the RIAA's protest is that the price of music is not just the cost of the plastic on which it's recorded, any more than the price of a movie is based on the cost of the film. In any event, dissatisfaction with the price is not a justification for stealing. Would you steal a book on the grounds that its price is too high? Or break into a theater because the tickets cost too much?

From the RIAA's point of view, the fact that CD sales were up in spite of the arrival of Napster is an irrelevance. In view of the then healthy state of the US economy, it would have been surprising if record sales had not increased. Common sense suggests that sales would have increased even more without Napster.

The CD market, said the RIAA, is not the only market at issue. Napster was also having an adverse effect on the ability of legitimate companies to deliver and market music online. Napster was interfering with the development of a legitimate music market on the Internet because it's very hard to sell music in competition with free copies of the same music on the same network. Even worse, Napster was devaluing music itself, teaching an entire generation that music is free and has no value. In short, it is hard to sell beer in a free bar.

Rosen goes back to the earlier issue that Napster were building a business on the backs of artists: "Cynics say the record industry doesn't like that model because it takes them out of the equation. And creating that demand for the music and the artist is very much a marketing and promotional function the record company does. The costs associated with that have to be absorbed somewhere."

The case, said the RIAA, would have important implications not just for online music, but for all copyright industries that are interested in launching legitimate businesses on the Internet. If a consumer were permitted to "share" with millions of anonymous strangers copyrighted music, motion pictures, software, books, photographs, or anything else just because he or she had bought a single copy of it, then copyright law as we know it would be turned upside down.

THE CASE FOR THE DEFENSE

The basis of Napster's defense was that the labels were trying to control their monopoly on record distribution. Milton E. Olin Jr, chief operating officer at Napster, claims that the major labels perceive Napster and companies like Napster, to be an enormous threat to their ability to maintain their dominance of the recording industry. This is because of their perceived potential to turn the way the recording industry, as dominated by the major labels, has traditionally operated completely upside down. To begin with, the major labels vocalized their view that if consumers are able to obtain music for free, they will refuse to pay for it in future and CD sales will drop.

In addition to fearing Napster, says Olin, the major labels also feared the Internet generally, for its potential to seriously adversely affect their ability to control the distribution of music. Indeed, this fear is the reason the major labels initially entirely resisted the idea of any digital distribution of music. It was only after Napster and other file sharing services popularized the notion of file sharing and digital distribution that the major labels were forced to recognize the vast potential of the Internet. They had only just realized that it serves as a powerful tool for the promotion and distribution of music – and that file sharing services like Napster posed a challenge to their domination of the industry.

From Napster's own point of view, it is an application that allows users to learn about others' musical tastes and share their MP3 files. If they choose to share files – and they are not required to – the application makes a list of the files designated by the user and sends the list to become part of the central Napster directory. The Napster directory is a list of all the files that members of the community are willing to share. This is accomplished by a file transfer from one person's computer directly to another's. They do this for no money, expecting nothing in return, on a person-to-person basis.

The argument, in a nutshell, is that Napster is an Internet directory service. Napster does not copy files. It does not provide the technology for copying files. Napster does not compress files. It does not transfer files. Napster simply facilitates communication. It is a throwback to the original structure of the Internet described above. Rather than building large servers, Napster relies on communication between the personal computers of the members of the Napster community. The information is distributed all across the Internet, allowing for a depth and a scale of information that is truly revolutionary.

The Napster method of person-to-person, non-commercial file sharing is a new tool, a new way of sharing information. All new tools change the way we do things, and that often upsets the established order. In the case of Napster, the established order is the recording and music publishing industry. When presented with this new tool, the industry reacted by attempting to crush Napster, as it has tried to do with other technologies in the past.

HERE COME THE HOT SHOTS: WHO IS DAVID BOIES?

David Boies is a hot-shot lawyer. A native of rural Illinois, he spent 30 years at the law firm Cravath, Swaine & Moore before setting up his own New York firm, Boies, Schiller & Flexner. David Boies probably can't tell the difference between Chuck D and Metallica, but cases where technology and the law come crashing together are among David Boies' specialties and Napster was certainly one of those. Boies rarely loses at trial and over the years has represented IBM, AOL, and CBS, but it was Boies' humiliation of Bill Gates and Microsoft and campaigning on behalf of the Gore team in the 2000 US election controversy that made him a legend. In between the two cases came Napster.

David Boies (see box above) says that there were two basic issues, and the recording industry would have to prove each of them in order to prevail. If Napster won on either of the two, he says, Napster should prevail.

Are Napster's users engaged in copyright infringement? If they are not, that's the end of the matter, because nobody alleges that Napster directly infringes any copyright.

When Napster's users engage in noncommercial sharing of music – noncommercial copying of music – is that activity copyright infringement?

Boies said not, for two basic reasons. The first is that this kind of noncommercial consumer copying is recognized as fair use under common-law theories and doctrines, and under the Supreme Court's criteria. And second, with respect to audio recordings – that is, music – the Audio Home Recording Act directly says that noncommercial copying by consumers is lawful. The 9th Circuit, in RIAA v. Diamond Multimedia Systems in 1999, read that statute as permitting all noncommercial consumer copying as lawful.

Napster and Boies argued that copyright is a tool of public policy. It does not vindicate a private right, said Boies: "Copyright is therefore an incentive that we as a society grant so that we may have better access to more original expression. In the end, the copyright laws are for the benefit of the public as a whole, not the individual copyright owners. The balance requires that these rights be limited so that we as a society can share, grow and build upon one another's creativity. But that balance is always at risk in the struggle between copyright absolutists and those who think more limited protections are appropriate."

Hank Barry, CEO of Napster, said, "Companies that hold copyrights on behalf of creators, and which control distribution of creative works, have a strong inclination to extend copyright into a complete monopoly control over the creative work – to change the copyright laws from a balanced vehicle for public enrichment to an unbalanced engine of control. As a result, copyright holders traditionally are reluctant to allow new technologies to emerge."

This, said Napster, was just part of the great march of technology through history. As a result of decisions made by Congress and the courts, technological advances like radio, the cassette recorder, cable television and the VCR have survived copyright holders' attacks and, in the end, proved to be a financial boon to these same concerned copyright holders. That this is true can be demonstrated by the statement made by Jack Valenti, the [octogenarian] president of the Motion Picture Association of America, in the context of the Sony Betamax litigation. At that time, he testified before Congress that the VCR was to the movie industry what "the Boston Strangler is to a woman alone." Sixteen years after Valenti's statement, the movie industry is thriving as never before. US box office receipts in 1999 reached $7.5 billion, their highest level ever. All of this in spite of an 85.1% VCR penetration rate in US households. By all accounts, the VCR has enormously helped the movie industry, and now accounts for more than half of the industry's revenues.

Barry continued, "It is my firm belief that the consumers who use Napster are not committing copyright violations. We disagree, and believe that the vast majority of Napster users appropriately operate in a non-commercial manner within the bounds of the copyright laws. Napster's view on this issue is based on a review of the copyright statutes, court decisions and the expert opinions of copyright scholars."

Napster relied on history to preserve its future. Furthermore, even if one were to assume that some Napster users were violating copyright law, Napster would still not be liable for any copyright infringement because of the landmark Sony Betamax decision. The Betamax case recognized that Sony's offering of the Betamax VCR did not constitute copyright infringement because the

Betamax was capable of non-infringing uses, such as copying for time-shifting purposes. Napster allows similar uses. For example, Napster users often transfer an MP3 file onto their hard drive as a complement to a CD they already own. In addition, studies show that Napster users share songs as a way to sample music before purchasing it, including music that the user would not normally consider buying. Finally, Napster provides a critical link between new artists and the public. Too much creative talent fails to get through the recording and music publishing industry filter. Lack of recording contracts and radio play should not deny creators from finding an audience. Napster is a great way for fans to find the music of artists they read about or hear played at clubs.

Why would you want to download an album and send it your friends? The fact that there has been an increase in CD sales despite the impact of file sharing programs such as Napster points to the fact that consumers do not view MP3 files as a satisfactory replacement for CDs for several reasons. For example, downloading an entire album is burdensome, the sound quality is inferior to that of CDs, there is an inconvenience to having a song only in MP3 format (most people have CD players in their homes, cars, etc), and an MP3 does not provide the tangible product – liner notes, pictures and, often, lyrics – that a CD does.

WHAT OTHER LAWYERS SAID AT THE TIME

"If Napster wins this, then presumably everybody that is propagating MP3 files and movie files will be protected," said attorney Carl Oppedahl, of Oppedahl & Larson. "And every time the music industry faces a technological change or an unfavorable ruling, they run to Congress to plug the latest hole in the dike."

But as the Napster case demonstrates, even relatively recent laws have not kept up with the rapid pace of technological advances. "The whole area of music on the Internet is a complicated one," said Jonathan Band, an attorney with law firm Morrison & Foerster in Washington, D.C. "All the new software could have been done by the record companies. But what you see is the industry trying to preserve the old model as opposed to taking advantage of the new model and being innovative and cutting-edge."

One of Napster's lawyers, Laurence Pulgram of Palo Alto, California-based Fenwick & West, has argued that his client falls under the law's safe harbor because its services are similar to Web browsers or other applications offered on the Web. "Napster does not control or supervise the materials transmitted between users in any way," Pulgram wrote in his legal papers. In the past, courts have almost always left it up to the copyright holder to enforce compliance, steering clear of clamping down on new technology. In the famous Sony case, for example, the US Supreme Court refused to block sales of VCRs. Today, the purchase of movie videotapes by consumers is one of the main sources of revenue for the film industry.

Others believe that exemptions to laws passed by Congress in the past were intended to protect Net access providers such as America Online, AT&T WorldNet and MCI WorldCom, and definitely not companies like Napster. "I don't know if Napster are going to be able to shoehorn themselves into an exemption in the DMCA (see box below)," said Neil Rosini, a lawyer at New York law firm Franklin, Weinrib, Rudell & Vassallo, who represents online music firm Myplay. "The defense is a novel one, but if Napster wins this, I predict the law will be rewritten in eight minutes ... The DMCA was never intended for companies like Napster."

WHAT DOES THE LAW SAY?

The Digital Millennium Copyright Act (DMCA), considered an important legislation for the entertainment industry, was written to protect Internet service providers from unknowingly hosting any illegal activities. For instance, you wouldn't blame a telecommunications company if two people plotted a bank robbery by talking over one of their lines. Even so, if an ISP is aware that it is being used to host illegal activity, it must take the site down as soon as possible. What often happens in practice though, is that MP3 pirate sites often simply disappear only to come back in a slightly different form a few months down the road.

GUILT TAX

In the United States, there is a 3% tax on the sales of blank digital tapes, cartridges and writable CDs. This is effectively a tax imposed for real or imagined piracy. One third of the tax goes into a "musical works fund" which is administered by a couple of federal agencies that distribute it to songwriters and music publishers. The rest goes to record companies, who then pass on 40% to their artists, while a portion goes to unknown artists. The redistribution is undeniably good for big-name artists, but it also makes those who pay the tax feel less guilty about ripping off music from the Internet.

At the heart of the dispute is the digital copyright law passed two years ago to expand online safeguards for software, literature and music. The law also shields Net access providers from liability. That important caveat places the copyright burden on the person using a legitimate service. In other words, much as Xerox can't be held liable for the actions of people who copy books, songs and artwork on its machines, online service providers can't be held responsible for the actions of their customers. But how lawmakers define service providers is open for broad interpretation, experts say.

WHAT THE JUDGES SAID

The judges were distinctly unimpressed by Napster's arguments. In a landmark ruling in February 2001, they upheld the decision of a lower court against Napster. Through "peer-to-peer" file sharing, it said, Napster allows users to make copyright music files stored on individual computer hard drives available for copying by other Napster users. Napster had broken the law through its technology. It searched for music files stored on other users' computers and allowed the transfer of exact copies of other users' music files from one computer to another via the Internet.

The judges agreed with the lower court that the record companies had presented a convincing case of direct copyright infringement by Napster users. The panel also agreed with the district court's rejection of Napster's defense

FREQUENTLY ASKED QUESTIONS

Doesn't the Audio Home Recording Act (AHRA) of 1992 in the US provide protection for Napster?

The AHRA covers devices designed or marketed for the primary purpose of making digital musical recordings, which are required to incorporate technology to prevent serial copying. General purpose computers, the court ruled, are not covered by the AHRA, so that statute imposes no obligations on Napster and provides no immunity for either Napster or its users. Even if general purpose computers were covered, the AHRA would not allow the widespread distribution of music that is enabled by Napster.

Is this similar to the motion picture association's battle against VCRs in the 1980s?

Yes, said Napster. Not at all, said the RIAA. A VCR can be used lawfully (time-shifting, rentals, home movies) and never infringe on a copyright. The overwhelming use of Napster, the court ruled, is for infringing purposes.

that its users were engaged in "fair use" of the copyright material. The judges also found that Napster could be liable for two types of copyright infringement under two doctrines: contributory copyright infringement and vicarious copyright infringement.

What does this mean? In terms of contributory copyright infringement, the judges said that Napter knowingly encouraged and assisted its users to infringe the record companies' copyrights and that Napster materially contributes to the infringing activity. As to the vicarious copyright infringement claim, the panel concluded that Napster has a direct financial interest in its users' infringing activity and retains the ability to police its system for infringing activity.

ROSEN CROWS

Following the ruling, Hilary Rosen and the record industry wasted no time in rubbing the judgment in: "They originally told the courts that the purpose of their system was to promote new artists. But they told their users that they could use their service to avoid ever having to wade through unknown artists again. Napster told the courts that they didn't have to pay artists or copyright owners. But they told the creative community, the press and the congress that they wanted to pay artists and copyright owners. They told the courts that they could not possibly determine what music was authorized and what music was infringing, saying it was technically impossible. Yet they made a deal with Bertelsmann to build an authorized system that would respect artists and copyright owners; and we know they have been meeting with numerous technology companies who can do the job."

Rosen offered an olive branch to the underground Internet: "We know you love music; so do we. Our member companies and the artists on whose behalf this case was brought work every day to create the most expressive, passionate, diverse and exciting music in the world. This is their promise to you. If you understand and respect their desire to continue making that music for you, they will assure you that you will still be able to use the most innovative technologies to listen to their work. This may be a turbulent transition but the promise for the future of music is great."

But the millions and millions of Napster users weren't really listening to the likes of Rosen...

CHAPTER 5

The Voice of the People: the Fury of the Underground Internet

INTRODUCTION

THE RECORD INDUSTRY'S ATTEMPTS to go after Napster were never going to win it any popularity contests. Indeed, their individual and collective lawsuits seemed to serve only to help the company do exactly what it needed to accomplish for long-term success – raising awareness of the service among a more demographically diverse group of potential users.

When big business got nasty, the writing was on the wall for Napster. But its drawn-out destruction in turn unleashed the fury of music lovers everywhere. These people in their millions loved the music to which Napster gave them access, the feeling of community it generated and the sense of empowerment that it gave them over big business.

The wrath of millions of fans spread rapidly through the underground Internet, via chat forums and message forums all across the medium. This chapter is devoted to articulating that wrath in the simplest way possible – by reporting the most incisive and interesting of these views. The views expressed here are highlights from an investigation of dozens of major chat rooms from all around the Net.

Just as the power of the underground Internet turned Napster into a powerhouse in the music industry, the power of public opinion will inevitably shape the attitude of artists and record companies for years to come. Such is the power of the underground Internet.

GREEDY RECORD COMPANIES

The wrath against the shutdown of Napster focused in two principal areas: record companies and anti-Napster artists. First, the record companies. Some of the brickbats have been very unpleasant indeed.

"It is high time the recording companies and artists started caring for and respecting the customers. They seem to be getting more arrogant and ruthless in their approach."

K, Singapore

Wake up and smell the coffee – people are fed up with being ripped off by a notoriously unpleasant and greedy music industry. I agree that artists should reap the rewards of their creativity, but let the staggering popularity of Napster be a long-overdue warning shot to profiteering music bosses!"

AS, UK

"I can't wait for online music distribution, where artists can sell their music for a fair price and not use the greedy record companies for a middleman."

PF, Alabama

"The record companies have been ripping customers off with huge profits for years, is it no wonder people resort to using Napster. The record companies are worried as they won't be able finance their extortionate lifestyles."

J, UK

"Record companies have many ways to avoid and delay paying artists they employ, so it's pretty hypocritical of them to use artists' intellectual property rights as the basis of their case. What will they call the Sony Bertallsman [sic] server – GREEDSTER?"

I, Canada

"It's absolutely shocking … large multi-national companies make millions of dollars every year ripping off not only consumers, but also their 'stars.' Napster provided an incredibly important outlet for music lovers and artists to 'reclaim' what they had lost under the control of large recording companies."

D, UK

THE PRICE ISN'T RIGHT

Why do Napster users seem so down on the record companies? The answer is summed up in one word – price.

"Many of the songs that can be found are not readily available in this neck of the woods and the performers are long gone, so could not collect royalties in any case. Yet the record companies make a lot of money selling those CDs at outrageous prices."

D, Canada

"If [the record companies] charged a reasonable price there would be little demand for Napster and in trying to close it down they are alienating their customers who will have even less compunction about using the next system that comes along."

AS, UK

"As long as CD prices are so unreasonably high, services like Napster will thrive."

N, UK

"If the music CDs were selling for two or three dollars there probably would not have been any music file sharing sites."

NC, USA

"The music industry is overpriced – if you buy a £15 CD and don't like it, then that's £15 wasted. If you download an MP3 and like the music, it is not such a waste of money to buy the legitimate CD. Does radio promote the buying of music, even though you can tape record it?"

M, Wales

GREEDY ARTISTS

Aside from the middlemen in the record industry, the recording artists that campaigned against Napster came in for heavy criticism.

"The best thing that Napster has done for all of us is brought certain musicians out into the light for what they really are. ... thanks to a couple of kids with a good idea, we now know that all they truly are are guys on commission, not rock stars, not artists who just want to make good music ... greedy artists take music to the lowest of the lower levels."

J, Michigan

"Napster is in no way a bad thing. I know that as a teenager, a great deal of my money goes directly into the music industry for things such as tickets, poster, CDs, singles and other things music inspired. So if ... the artists want to start charging every time you preview or listen to music online, they can just get the hell over it. Unlike them, I have a certain amount that I can spend on music and sorry, it's not my whole paycheck."

DN, Illinois

"It happens: deal with it. It just means you need to have more concerts and other means of making your millions. Sorry for the pay cut, guys."

BB, California

"I thought that all musicians wanted was for people to enjoy their music, but I'll never believe those words again."

D, California

"A true rock star is a person who is doing what they love and doesn't care about how much they earn. Napster is just something stars can place their blame on when nobody buys their CD. Maybe they should be spending more time working on their music, instead of a petty lawsuit."

T, Western Australia

"Any musician that supports the shutdown of Napster is a hypocrite. The reason people become musicians is because they want to share their music with others ... All these musicians need to stop being greedy. If they really want to whine about not getting money, they should start whining to their record company, who is the one who is truly screwing them over."

G, California

"At last I can sleep at night knowing that Britney can afford another aeroplane."

T, UK

NEVER MIND THE QUALITY ...

Just as record companies set the price levels of CDs, artists set the quality levels. The consensus of views seems to be that the latter, like the former, leaves much to be desired. Furthermore, those artists who complain most loudly about copyright infringement are, according to the underground, those most likely to be lacking in talent.

"I am a regular Napster user, but I will still go out and buy a record if there are two or three songs that I like on it ... Maybe artists who do

not do so already will have to start producing records full of quality music as opposed to relying on one hit single to make them rich and famous."

T, New York

"The point with Napster is to get the music you want without having to pay the price of a whole useless CD with only one song you like. More artists should make singles."

J, Florida

METALLICA AND DR DRE

Two artists at the forefront of the challenge to Napster have been Dr Dre and Metallica. The latter, and in particular the group's drummer, Lars Ulrich, has come in for some savage criticism.

"You know how Dr Dre said that it's like working and not getting a paycheck? Well, if you don't like it, get a new job."

B, Indiana

"I guess people like Metallica and the RIAA have once again succeeded in blocking out different kinds of music, forcing the public to swallow down whatever crap they shove at us."

FS, Oregon

"I think the police ... should get a search warrant to execute a full-on search on Lars Ulrich's house for various copyright infringements, like bootleg concert tapes, then prosecute him to the fullest extent of the law. I bet ten to one that he has a few burned disks and games on his computer himself."

B, British Columbia

Not everyone agrees on this, however.

IRRESISTIBLE FORCES

"People are calling Metallica and other anti-Napster artists greedy. None of these people were apparently listening when Lars Ulrich said Metallica were spending way more money on lawyers' fees than Napster was taking from them. Metallica are losing money fighting Napster, yet people are calling them greedy."

KO, Michigan

COURTS WRONG

Many think the various court rulings are simply wrong for a variety of reasons.

"Holding Napster responsible for illegal downloads is like holding Peugeot responsible if someone driving it ignores a traffic signal. This is just another case of powerful corporations bending legal rulings to suit themselves. It's not a logical extension of any true justice."

PJC, USA

"This is of course a sad day. It's the day music died; killed by a judge. Copyright infringement has always been going on, without being seen or heard of. If the court thinks it's fair, then can it just order the non-use of blank tapes and videos? Napster as research said, helped the progress of the music industry, not the other way round."

MAE, Egypt

"I went to the library, and found tons of CDs to burn in my player. So why don't they stop the makers of the burners and stop the libraries?"

Treega, USA

"I had my birthday and got a CD burner. ... I wanted it because I love music and the computer, so I got it so I could burn CDs off of Napster ... So now all the money for the burner and the system have gone down the drain. What a great birthday, huh?"

AL, USA

"Napster as a community of users has now been forced underground. It's going to change into something the record companies have no chance of ever policing."

C, UK

WHY ATTACK SOMETHING THAT DOESN'T DO ANY HARM?

Aside from those Napster users that are furious at what they perceive as the greed of the record companies and artists.

"The arrival of the domestic tape recorder all those years ago didn't exactly achieve the end of the music industry. People have been doing tapes for their friends for years and all it's done is increase awareness of an artist's music. Why is Napster any different? Just because the quality is a little better? Pfah! So what? Theft of music? I don't think so!"

DG, UK

"I suppose blank tapes and videos will be banned next so we can't copy anything. The vast majority of Napster users never do anything commercial with their MP3s. However, if something like this is free, in the eyes of giant corporations it has to be a bad thing, as everyone can afford to go out and pay £3.99 for CD singles, can't they?"

RS, England

"I have used it to download a track I have heard part of on the radio. If, on re-hearing it, I still like the track I purchase the CD online. This is no worse than recording tracks off the radio."

C, UK

"No Napster = no music for the common man. There is going to be no drastic increase in sales of CDs if Napster were shut down. It would only leave behind a lot of disappointed people who just have no music of their choice to listen to."

PK, USA

NAPSTER IS GOOD FOR MOST ARTISTS

A large part of the bewilderment at the move to close Napster down is that it has given many young artists a chance for exposure that they may never have had if their only outlet for listening to music had been related to the tastes of record company executives.

"Sites like Napster bring much needed publicity to unsigned artists who work harder than the greedy pop stars who are causing all the fuss."

S, England

"I've been using AudioGalaxy rather than Napster and I've bought 10 CDs in the last 4 weeks by artists I had not heard of that were introduced to me as being similar to those for which I had demonstrated a liking. I've also started listening to other genres. Surely this is a good thing!"

MW, UK

"The ability to listen to [music] I had not previously supported on Napster led me this year to purchase approximately nine CDs I would not have normally purchased from listening to mainstream

radio play, watching MTV or VH1, and from reading music reviews in various publications."

MW, California

"What about the artists that agree with what Napster is doing? Why aren't they speaking up?"

T, Pennsylvania

NAPSTER HELPS RECORD COMPANIES

Many others simply can't understand why the record companies have got it in for Napster when the file-swapping service has helped them so much.

"Napster usage grew from 20,000 to 50,000,000 in one year. In the same time period, album sales grew by a massive 10% in the UK and the States. There is a direct link. Please don't be fooled by the majors who are willingly shooting themselves in the foot and blowing away the most potent marketing tool ever created."

AH, UK

"The talk of lost royalties is ridiculous. Ageing musicians are failing to understand the Internet. When good music gets heard, albums are sold. Nobody claims to lose money when their music is played on the radio. And to prove it, album sales are actually higher this year than last."

MF, UK

"Personally I think Napster has encouraged me to buy more CDs than I normally would have by listening to bands which I normally wouldn't listen to. If anyone loses out on the ruling, it's the record companies. The rest of us will simply go through other avenues."

H, USA

"Programs like Napster should be seen as a selling tool by the record companies. If the user likes what they hear the chances are they will go out and buy the full product."

T, UK

"Napster has given us the chance to listen and appreciate artists we would never have listened to before. We have then purchased their CDs. Simply, Napster has benefitted us and the record companies."

S, Germany

"I will definitely buy some more CDs ... It is a great feeling rushing home to listen to the latest from your favorite band or artist. That gets lost while you're waiting for the MP3 to download."

C, Pennsylvania

NAPSTER'S GREAT FOR PARENTS

There are some people who like Napster for reasons that are unrelated to the rights and wrongs of song-swapping.

"As a parent, I appreciate being able to listen to what my kids listen to. Having the MP3 files to listen to makes a big difference in the CDs my kids are allowed to purchase."

Anonymous

"Napster is fun. It has made my young daughter computer literate."

PW, Australia

AND IT'S REALLY GOOD FOR ALL SORTS OF WEIRD STUFF

Most people love Napster not so that they can get hold of the latest Britney

Spears CD, but so that they can find all sorts of weird stuff that can't find elsewhere – least of all through the record companies.

"When I purchase a musical recording, I am paying for a license to listen to that music, and surely that license lasts a lifetime. Many of my earlier purchases – some dating back to the 1960s – are in poor condition. Unfortunately, there is no way to go to the local music shop and buy replacement media without paying the license fee over again. Fortunately, today's technology has allowed me to replace the medium on which the music is recorded and Napster has played a vital part in that."

DH, England

"It proved to be the only method that allowed me to download songs sung even 90 years ago, which I otherwise couldn't have found."

MM, Greece

"I experimented with Napster and found defects in many records such as premature endings and extraneous sounds. My time spent reviewing and editing to burn a quality CD is worth more than the cost of a new commercial CD. So I say leave Napster alone. It's good for sampling and for finding 'out of print' stuff."

D, USA

I think this could be a case of the record companies winning the battle, but losing the war. The strength of Napster is that you can find rare or limited release tracks. Make these widely available and Napster is probably dead.

J, Canada

One of the main strengths of Napster is the ability to obtain hard to find or out of press music. Will the corporate MP3 sites offer tracks by General Surgery, Narcosis, Old Funeral or Funebre?

J, UK

GREAT BUT WRONG

If you didn't care about Napster, you probably wouldn't bother to post a message in a chat room. But there are plenty of people who feel that while Napster is a great thing, Shawn Fanning and his friends are ultimately in the wrong.

"Napster should get axed. Okay, it's a really cool program that allows people to download music … [but] musicians like me don't find this the greatest thing, because of the fact that it makes us lose out. I mean everything is good only to a certain limit. This is way beyond that."

Z, Australia

"I don't think it was [Napster's] intention to screw both bands out of money. What I disagree with is how Napster has dealt with the situation. I've worked in the music industry and I know how much money bands make from CDs, merchandise etc. What most of the general public doesn't realize is how much money the record labels make off these bands."

JE, Illinois

"If a band doesn't want their work on Napster, then it should be immediately taken off. Metallica and Dr Dre have every right to be pissed off … I knew from the beginning when I heard about Napster that it was going to fall right on its face and it did."

JH, Wisconsin

"Quite a few people are really missing the point. If people decided not to pay for music anymore, how would musicians be able to record music? They would not be able to."

Anonymous

"Napster is great hands down. But what they are doing is very illegal. They are like an illegal radio station. My friend and his brother

haven't bought a CD in two years because of Napster ... Ask anyone on the street what they think and they will say Napster is right, Metallica is wrong."

AB, Maryland

"In principle I agree with the court because usually you have to pay for music and companies/artists are losing money. On the other hand most top musicians do earn a hell of a lot of money. Some less well known artists claim they can't earn a living because of the Napster program but they have got to remember that most songs downloaded are of the popular kind which have been written by rich artists. At the end of the day I'm more in favor of Napster but I do understand the court ruling."

KZ, UK

COPYRIGHT RIGHT

Others feel that the enforcement of copyright is a far more important issue than the fate of Napster.

"Me! Me! Me! Greedy! Greedy! Greedy! That's all I hear on both sides of this argument: from the Napster users and from the artists. Yes there is copyright infringement going on. Yes, illegal stuff is happening and Napster's part of it ... that's right! It's the law: that's how it works. Deal with it or phone your local representative to get her to work to amend the Copyright Act. But before you do, don't forget that the copyright laws in this country were created to protect and foster artistic expression for the public (that's you) good."

M, Texas

"I would support Napster if they at least would get the artists' permission before making songs accessible. Some artists have

*said that unfinished songs were being traded. That's ridicu-
lous!"*

T, Montana

*"I am happy that someone finally has shut Napster down. The law
states that copyrighted material cannot be sold in anyway, shape, or
form. That includes online! Churches have been slapped with fines
because they would photocopy a hymn."*

H, Missouri

*"Music doesn't just happen: it is the product of somebody's imagina-
tion and hard work, not a natural resource like water or air. Artists
whose music is enjoyed by others should be paid for what they create."*

SK, UK

NAPSTER HYPOCRISY

Others think that those who run Napster are quite simply hypocrites.

*"Napster is a trademark. Remember The Offspring selling T-shirts
with the Napster logo? Where are those shirts now? Napster Inc.
demanded they be taken down. Immediately. Why? The Offspring
was violating copyrights that Napster itself was violating. Who is
to protect Napster when Napster violates what they treasure? ...
Sorry folks, you've been had. Laws protect everyone, not just the more
popular guy, or the weaker kid ... So who's right? A company started
by two 18-year-olds or a justice system that has been efficient for
over 220 years? That little "c" in a circle means something ... If you
want to try out the music, go to a record store and listen to it, or, by
golly, listen to the radio."*

E.G., North Carolina

"Why should music be free? Nothing else in the world is free. Why should a musician work for free? ... it is [Napster's] fault. They should have contacted the artists and asked their permission, plain and simple ... Guess what? I'd like to buy a Porsche, but can't afford it!! Does that mean I go down to my local Porsche dealer and drive off with one anyway? ... Many people ignorantly state that a CD costs less than a quarter to produce. This is true ... but do you have any idea how much it costs to record an album? ... you're shafting a bunch of regular people just like you and me who are just trying to get by. Good job."

Z, Maryland

"It is theft, a lack of morals, and lack of common respect, yet because people want to get the easy way out and not be forced to pay for the music, the artists themselves are labeled 'the bad guys'. I think not."

EA, Texas

"You're being scammed by Napster, people. They are turning it into a money issue knowing full well that they were in the wrong from the get-go."

SJ, New England

"Metallica and Dr. Dre have the right to be angry at Napster. These extremely creative individuals have devoted their lives to their art and are entitled to every single red cent for their creations. ... All of you Napster users can do me a favor. Get a job, make some money and use that money to buy all of the CDs you want. Nothing in life comes for free."

C, Minnesota

"If I had a CD burner, I would never go to the music store. Why would I spend $17 on something I can get for free? But I don't have

one and I don't use Napster. Why? Because musicians have the right to do whatever they please with their products."

L, Missouri

"Let's say you work a long ten-hour day at the office. At the end of the day, some jack-ass (in this hypothetical scenario, let's call him "Crapster") goes to your boss with all your work and says, 'Hey Boss, look at all the work I did today!' Essentially, this is what Napster is doing."

DN, Texas

"How does (did) Napster help artists reclaim their music from the faceless industry giants? If they're being ripped off by the corporations paying them meager mechanical royalties, surely removing even this source of income doesn't help?"

PM, UK

"I can't believe anyone thinks Napster is about anything but money. They don't care about 'free access' and 'sharing' they want to make a buck on someone else's work."

DH, Canada

"Napster claims that they are helping musicians sell records by allowing fans to 'test-drive' the record before buying it. That's fine, if they have the band's permission. However, what Napster does now is no different than someone test-driving a car without the dealer's consent. It's theft – even if you intend to buy it. ... what about new bands who haven't even made enough to pay back their record label? These bands will get dropped if they don't sell records. By using Napster, you're poopin' where you eat and screwing those you love."

VB, Pennsylvania

GENIE OUT OF THE BOTTLE

An overwhelming number of people think that the whole Napster debate is in many ways irrelevant. Whether its Napster, Nepster or Nipster, file sharing is a fact of life and always will be, whatever the courts decide.

"We all knew this was coming and it is unfortunate. There was on-line file sharing before Napster and there still will be afterwards. ... it's not the end of the world. If Dr. Dre, Metallica and the recording industry are stupid enough to think that they have 'won', maybe they'll shut the hell up for a little while."

JG, California

"You will never stop digital music. As long as there is the Internet, music will be made and distributed in a manner that is more illegal than Napster. Napster will not go quietly into the night."

J, Minneapolis

"Shutting down Napster is not the solution to this problem ... then they can use technology to send their music to everybody. They need to stop fighting the technology and use it instead."

MW, Virginia

"Bands like Metallica and Dr. Dre aren't trying to stop the inevitable progress of music and media. We'll be seeing this exact same debate over movies and such in the next few years. It doesn't matter if Napster is shut down; people still have a million other sources to get MP3s from. ... I think the real solution is for record companies to either find a way to work with technology, or give consumers more incentive to buy music. CDs today are way overpriced. I'd like to see more bands put out DVD albums or CD-ROMs, where the actual CD could be used for much more than music ... That would be a good way to evolve with technology."

CC, California

"MP3 is bigger than just Napster. I've been getting MP3s off the Internet since before Napster was even created and if Napster closes, then I'm still going to get MP3s for free from other places ... What about Gnutella? There is no centralized server and no one to shut down! They can't stop Gnutella and they can't stop MP3!"

RD, New York

"Give the public a little more credit. If they really want to share their music files, they don't need Napster to do it. Napster was a great convenience, sure, but if it's gone, the public will find another way."

B, Pennsylvania

"I agree that the music industry might have won this battle but they have started a war; a war against technology itself. Their action will only trigger us to resort to other sites in the future."

KF, Japan

"Whether or not Napster survives, the technology is now out there – and other Napster clones will get popular."

H, USA

"Shutting Napster down will not remove the problem – there are already Napster clone clients that can connect to Napster clone servers. When Napster goes down smart users will simply switch to a free alternative."

AA, UK

"The record industry cannot win against technology. Stopping Napster will ironically do more harm than good, as it would have been much easier to try to work with Napster, than to force its users to the untraceable underground."

MC, UK

"As someone who worked for one of the big producers, I can tell you they have been working on downloadable formats for a long time. Unfortunately due to the inherent stupidity of top level management these downloadable music formats are generally four to five times larger than their MP3 equivalents."

BH, England

BLATANT DISREGARD

Not only are people saying that the genie is out of the bottle, but that they will completely ignore any rulings, no matter how important the people who make them.

"The world is evolving and so are the people. We no longer live in a world where we are confined to the rules and regulations of those with pockets much larger than ours ... I had planned to hit the mall this weekend to pick up the Layzie Bone and Lil' Kim CDs. Now thanks to [attempts to close down Napster], I am more than happy to skip it and hack off of some sites."

RM, Ontario

"There are many other 'Napsters', many other methods of down-loading free music, and there always will be. People in growing numbers are realizing that we don't have to be slaves to huge multinationals who get to define legality as they see fit. Napster lives."

NR, Australia

YOU'RE ALL MAD

Of course there are always those who think that everybody else has got it all wrong.

"Why don't you stop wasting your time about all this Napster crap and start worrying about the music industry? Pop music is taking over! Instead of boycotting Metallica, Dr. Dre and the RIAA, why don't you boycott Backstreet Boys and Britney Spears, cause their music sucks!"

JS, New Jersey

"Who said the American courts had jurisdiction over the entire globe (much as they like to think this is the case)? What's to stop competitors or even Napster itself moving to another country?"

T, UK

"I don't use Napster because it's free – I use it because it's a massively more CONVENIENT method of accessing the music I want to hear. In many instances, it is also the ONLY method I have of accessing the music I want to hear."

MA, UK

"I think it is a disgrace that something that has actually resulted in increased CD sales is being forced offline, and yet there are thousands of pornographic and pedophilic websites online and apparently immune from justice."

JP, UK

ANSWERS

Finally, a few have turned their attention to solutions and the emerging consensus is that there has to some sort of subscription service.

The whole Napster thing doesn't just have to do with artists being greedy. In an article I read, a guy who ran a CD store would just look at the CDs and then go download them on Napster ... the best solution would be for record companies to find a way to preventing

CDs from being ripped, charge less for CDs and make music available online at fair prices."

Anonymous, Florida

"Napster should be allowed to charge a subscription, which should support the artists, and them alone."

AS, UK

"I feel Napster should put a membership fee on its service. This would get rid of the lawsuits filed against it and the money hungry artists will not have to complain that people are getting their music for free. If people want to share the music they own I feel that they should be allowed."

M, UK

"This has to be good for music in the long run, and there is no reason why it should not be economically sustainable for record companies as well. The majors should follow BMG's lead and direct their energies toward a new, sustainable model of distribution, rather than wasting their time and money trying to stem an unstoppable force."

MA, UK

CHAPTER 6

Bertelsmann (and the End of Napster As We Know It)

INTRODUCTION

A S THE UNDERGROUND INTERNET RAGED in one direction and the record companies in another, Bertelsmann was notable by its absence from the debate over Napster. To outsiders, this seemed a ridiculous state of affairs. Bertelsmann had a huge financial stake in music with Bertelsmann Music Group
(BMG) a quarter of the Bertelsmann empire with revenues of nearly $5 billion
and 12,000 employees. Furthermore, it was selling over half of its records into
the US market, Napster's home territory. Yet somehow their attitude to Napster wasn't quite in keeping with the other record labels. While Bertelsmann
maintained a level of public hostility to Napster over copyright issues, it soon
became clear that its attitude to the young upstart as a business proposition
was somewhat different.

Some senior executives at Bertelsmann had begun to think the unthinkable. File sharing was obviously a success, just as Shawn Fanning had predicted. It was a success because it was what customers wanted and because the
Napster technology was easy to use. And whatever else happened, there was
absolutely nothing that Bertelsmann or any other record company could do to
alter that fact. These thoughts led some at Bertelsmann to want to get to know
Napster better, rather than to fight it tooth and nail.

The evolution of a new attitude within Bertelsmann was not without its
problems. There was much internal resistance within Bertelsmann to even
talking with Napster.

THE STRUGGLE FOR "NEW" BERTELSMANN

To understand the mentality of Bertelsmann involves getting inside the minds of two of its executives: Thomas Middelhoff and Andreas Schmidt. Their pro-Napster sentiments went against the grain of conventional record company thinking and really got up the noses of their competitors.

Middelhoff brought Bertelsmann kicking and screaming into the twenty-first century – just in the nick of time. Under him, Bertelsmann has become more global and more diverse. Middelhoff himself often speaks of the "new Bertelsmann," not just a convenient adjective for repackaging purposes, but shorthand for the company's transition to a modern media company. His colleagues say that he always appears to be one move ahead of the opposition. For example, he was obsessed with the possibilities of digital streaming before most of his counterparts had any idea what it meant.

Although he may have the stereotypical dress sense of a Frankfurt banker, colleagues and friends say that Middelhoff is a man of surprising charm, easy humor and sense of perspective. "Thomas can defuse the tension in any room," says Aydin Caginalp, Bertelsmann's US lawyer for nearly twenty years. Maybe this is something which may be explained by his "hometown" lifestyle outside of work: he lives on a farm outside Gutersloh (the home town of Bertelsmann) with his wife, five children, 45 cows and sheep, and a duck pond.

Middelhoff's career took off on the back of a gamble that paid off spectacularly well. In 1995, shortly after he was named head of corporate strategy, Middelhoff persuaded the financially cautious Bertelsmann board to gamble $50 million on a 5% stake in a young Internet company called America Online. It was a masterstroke. The $50 million turned into $1.8 billion windfall and propelled him to the forefront of the Bertelsmann hierarchy. This was not really the lucky gamble it may seem. A year earlier Middelhoff had spent a year in the US trying to get to know all the leading players in the technology market and spotted the potential of AOL through his close friendship with AOL chief executive officer Steve Case.

Once in charge as chief executive at Bertelsmann, Middelhoff had been anxious to restructure the group and make greater use of the Internet to sell content, which was reflected by the controversial deal with Napster. Middelhoff was keen to give the company a new character and place his own people in the key areas. So in came Andreas Schmidt. Schmidt, now the head of Bertelsmann's e-commerce group, calls himself a journalist, but his life has been a lot more varied than that. He was at one time a soldier in the German border patrol but left the military after losing hearing in one ear due to an accident with a hand grenade. His great talent is to spot projects just ripe for the mass market, then pushing them really hard.

Schmidt, too, is a man of energy and humor. "I liken him to the energizer bunny," Caginalp told the New York Post. "He is nonstop. Time does not exist for him." Caginalp said he believed the remarkable thing about Schmidt is his ability to "maintain his eveness – he doesn't yell, he doesn't shout. He's always happy. You could wake him at two o'clock in the morning, tell him the world has gone to pot and within 10 minutes, he'll have you laughing."

Both men were coming to the same conclusion about the irresistible momentum behind file sharing developing as a result of Napster. "I realized that we had to pursue music from two sides," Middlelhoff said mid-way through 2000. "There is content, but there is also online file sharing. We could not get ahead without file sharing." Bertelsmann's technology arm had been working on its own file-sharing system for months. "But we realized that all the technology gave us was an illegal way to distribute files," said Middelhoff. "We had to make it legitimate, and Napster already had a base to work from."

Schmidt, meanwhile, had spent 80% of his working life on the road, thousands of miles from his wife and children in Germany. But his frequent telephone calls home made him realize that his own children were devoted Napster fans. It was easy, quick and had every music track you could ever hope to find. With Napster taking over, literally, in his own back yard, how could Schmidt ignore the potential of file sharing?

For both Middelhoff and Schmidt, therefore, Napster became a natural pathway to a longstanding pledge to make Bertelsmann the number one player in music content. To even talk to Napster was bound to annoy the other record companies intensely. Ironically, however, finding the courage to make the first move had been inspired by one of the other majors. Middelhoff decided to go after Napster following a meeting with Seagram chairman Edgar Bronfman Jr., a staunch enemy of Napster, in which they discussed ways to resolve the Napster question. "We walked out of Edgar's office, and Thomas and I looked at each other, and it just clicked," says Schmidt.

The same day, Schmidt got on the phone to Napster CEO Hank Barry and began eight weeks of "on–off" transcontinental negotiations. Discussions took place in San Francisco, Miami, New York City and even Bertelsmann's base in Gutersloh, Germany. Napster, for its part, was intrigued but initially very wary over Bertelsmann's advances. Barry called the two months of negotiations "an intense process."

Any business person will tell you that deal-making very often comes down to the personal chemistry of those facing each other across the negotiating table. Barry quickly formed a personal bond with Schmidt over what they both believed was an irresistible momentum in the area of file sharing. Schmidt's technological background impressed the Napster team. They first met in Palo Alto where the talking was done in the local Starbucks. Says Barry, "We talked in Miami, when Thomas [Middelhoff] was there for a conference. We spent time in Palo Alto at Stanford's campus, just roaming the grounds. We talked while walking through Central Park. We did our best talking when we removed ourselves from the conference room. Andreas was always driven and full of an entrepreneurial spirit."

Shawn Fanning was invited along to meet the Bertelsmann people and Thomas Middelhoff tried to persuade him that the two men had a lot more in common than being on opposite sides of the litigation process. It was early September 2000. "I had to explain the Bertelsmann culture and the Internet, the speed at which everything is changing and the importance of our similar thinking about the value of membership communities," recalled Middelhoff. For his part, Fanning was surprised that Middelhoff's views were pretty close to his own and he quickly became convinced that he could trust the German.

Less convinced, however, were others inside Bertelsmann. The brokering of the deal caused Bertelsmann to lose two of its most senior staff. Michael Dornemann, chairman, and Strauss Zelnick, president and CEO of BMG, announced five days after the Napster deal that they were quitting the company over concerns about its future strategy. Dornemann in particular had been considered a rival to Middelhoff in the battle for the seat of chief operating officer. Zelnick had been in charge of the entertainment department in New York.

Schmidt's original plan to do a deal with Napster had set off a high-level spat within Bertelsmann. Napster and BMG were close to settling on 2nd

October – the time when oral arguments in the music industry's case against the service were due to be heard – when talks were called off at the last minute on Zelnick's orders. Only at this stage were Zelnick and others invited to join the negotiations with Napster's Hank Barry and Shawn Fanning.

Underneath it all, Zelnick was fighting a desperate rearguard action alongside Dornemann, although the public comments were sweet enough. Talking to the *New York Post*,[1] Schmidt said of Zelnick, "I have the highest respect for Strauss… He was in a difficult position, coming from the record company perspective. He had to have a different view than the overall company. But really, we got along. We couldn't have done the deal without him." As for Schmidt, Zelnick said, "you've got to give him credit – he got the deal done. Andreas is smart, focused has tremendous energy and a wonderful sense of humor."

When the deal finally arrived, Zelnick tried some humor of his own. "We're still not on Napster's side," said Zelnick, laughing, when the deal was announced. "We're suing Napster. But we are also on the side of creating an array of legitimate distribution alternatives."

But five days later both Zelnick and Dornemann had left Bertelsmann.

THE MOMENT WHEN FILE SHARING AND BUSINESS GOT TOGETHER

It was on Halloween 2000 that the illegal but hugely popular Napster file sharing program met head on with the world of big business. The announcement of a strategic alliance between Bertelsmann and Napster sent shock waves around the world. To record companies, it signaled betrayal by one of their number in dealing with perceived mass infringement of copyright. To millions of users, it signaled betrayal of an idyllic dream of free and unlimited music on tap. But most importantly, it was the day when everybody realized that the potential of file sharing, in the music industry and beyond, was simply too big for businesses to ignore as a commercial tool.

The crux of the deal was the formation of a strategic alliance between Bertelsmann and Napster to develop the latter's file sharing service. Bertelsmann and Napster would, the former claimed, "provide Napster community members with high quality file sharing that preserves the Napster experience while at the same time providing payments to rightsholders, including recording artists, songwriters, recording companies and music publishers."[2]

Under the terms of the agreement, Napster was obliged to implement a new membership-based service. In return it was agreed that Bertelsmann would withdraw its lawsuit against Napster and make its music catalog available. Bertelsmann would then provide a loan to Napster to enable development of the new service. Crucially, Bertelsmann would hold a warrant to acquire a portion of Napster's equity. To help Napster overcome the enormous technological hurdles involved, Bertelsmann opened a $50 million line of credit to facilitate the company's development. The new Napster was expected to make payments to major labels, songwriters and independent artists.

Announcing the deal, Thomas Middelhoff acknowledged the incredible impact that file sharing had already had on the music business. Middelhoff admitted, "Person-to-person file sharing has captured the imagination of millions of people worldwide with its ease of use, global selection of content, and community features. Napster has pointed the way for a new direction for music distribution, and we believe it will form the basis of important and exciting new business models for the future of the music industry. We invite other record and publishing companies, artists and other industry members to participate in the development of secure and membership-based services."

At the same time Hank Barry said, "This strategic alliance with Bertelsmann is the right next step for Napster. The Napster community – which is the fastest-growing in the history of the Internet – will benefit enormously from Bertelsmann's historic commitment to innovation and its experience in offering a seamless and convenient user experience." The truth of the matter, however, was that with so many lawsuits pending, Napster had little choice other than to do a deal.

Underneath the nice press release sentiment, a battle for hearts and minds was being waged furiously. Middelhoff recognized that the deal may have been a bombshell to the outside world and not least to the other major record companies. So Middelhoff started to work the phones. The German giant appealed to the stunned other major labels suing Napster – Warner Music Group, EMI, Sony and Universal – to join the effort to develop the Napster

MIDDELHOFF, BERTELSMANN AND NAPSTER
IN A NUTSHELL

In mid-November 2000, Bertelsmann CEO Thomas Middelhoff gave a short question and answer session to *Business Week* magazine following the announcement of the deal between Bertelsmann and Napster. It serves as a useful summary of Middelhoff's views on a very complex deal.

Q: So far, the music industry has been trying to kill Napster. Now, you're embracing it. Why?

A: We have to deal with file sharing. We can't criminalize 37 million users. We have to develop business models that are legal. Somebody has to take the lead for the industry.

Q: Napster users aren't used to having to pay for music. How will you change that?

A: We're looking at a subscription-based model, a digital-download service. Subscribers in a first step would pay a fixed amount of money. We will give the money back to companies, publishers, and artists.

Q: What will happen to litigation against Napster by you and others in the industry?

A: If Napster realizes our requirements, we are ready to settle our litigation. We're inviting all the other music companies to join.

Q: What are the chances they will?

A: I've talked to other media companies, though I don't want to give their names. I hope they will agree. It's not easy. There is a lot of emotion between Napster and the music industry. We will know very soon whether they will accept it. Right now, we have something on the table.

Q: Was the negotiating process difficult?

A: [The Napster people] are "Robin Hoods." But my Internet experience [as a former board member of America Online] helped a lot. Andreas Schmidt [Bertelsmann's head of e-commerce] really bridged the gap. This is really his deal.

Source: *Business Week*

network. Stunned too, was Hilary Rosen over at the Recording Industry Association of America (RIAA), the powerful trade group representing the major labels. Rosen, however, later issued a statement in which she welcomed the deal as a step forward along the road to a legal business model for file sharing.

WHAT'S IN IT FOR BERTELSMANN?

With Napster besieged by lawsuits, it is easy to see the appeal of an olive branch from Bertelsmann. But why should Napster be of such appeal to Bertelsmann? Anyone looking for an answer to this question could do a lot worse than look at the thoughts of Thomas Middelhoff as expressed in a conference as early as August 2000 in Cologne.[3] While still working towards a secret deal with Napster, Middelhoff left a few clues to others about his feeling towards Napster and the whole phenomenon that it had created.

In his speech, Middelhoff pointed out two things that Napster clearly was not. Napster, in his eyes, was not a competitor in the traditional sense. In fact it wasn't really anything new at all. In former times, he noted, people exchanged records and recorded them onto cassettes. Instead, Napster was being used to exchange music virtually and thus achieve a completely new and global dimension.

Neither was Napster "magic" in any sense. As soon as it had found out about Napster, Bertelsmann's technology department had conducted an experiment to simulate the Napster software. In the event, it took them less than a day to develop a Napster-like server and, Middelhoff claimed, they could have gone online with it on the same day.

So why didn't they? Well, the unique feature of Napster, claimed Bertelsmann, was neither an ingenious technological achievement, nor a traditional business model that can be approached with the tools of the market. Instead the appeal of Napster was the idea that it could make music accessible in an uncomplicated way. Indeed in their online manifesto, Napster had set themselves themselves up as a Robin Hood of the music scene. Napster's own blurb said "technology is again the means for liberation. Join us in our fight to rebuild the music industry and return music to the people!"

Inspite of their copyright infringements, Middelhoff could see why Napster was so popular. In his Cologne speech, he admitted, "Let's be honest. Despite all of the dangers, Napster is pretty cool. It's an excellent music brand with the following characteristics: high quality, free delivery of music directly into your home, simple use, global selection from the repertory of all labels, prompt service and uncoupled program selection."

If the music industry failed to react, reasoned Middelhoff, it would lead in the mid-term to a collapse of traditional business models. With such a stark alternative, the music companies have no choice. "We have to be clear about one thing – regardless of whether or not Napster is allowed to continue, the system of file sharing will always be around. The music industry is challenged to turn it into a legal business."

Neverthless, Bertelsmann was the first major record industry to admit that it's continued existence would not in the short term be terminally damaged by the arrival of Napster, as one or two of the other record labels had claimed. Middelhoff admitted, "The music industry, of course, will not go down due to the Internet. And I'm not saying that with calculated optimism. The Internet needs content. And this content is generated by the media enterprises, that is, the newspaper and magazine publishers, the book publishers, the movie and television industry and the music industry." To keep this flow of content going, said Middelhoff, the music industry has to remember its core competency – and rediscover it: "Only then will it experience good fortune. And this core competency includes the discovery and development of musical talents and the promotion, distribution and marketing of their music – in the end, bringing the best music to the fans is the core competency of the music companies."

The music companies should go back on the offensive, said Middelhoff, and be open-minded towards new trends and innovative in their adoption of new technologies. It was important, he said, to understand the Internet as a new carrier medium and an addition to the familiar ones and to adapt business models, marketing concepts and technological strategies to the new medium. The goal, he said, must be to deliver music to its customers – regardless of which channels were used.

How would Middelhoff and the other record companies make this happen? Bertelsmann could launch an online file sharing business right away although whether anyone would use it would be a matter of debate. Similarly, said Middelhoff, the music labels had to make an all-out effort to digitize their music and publish their entire catalogs online. It was therefore imperative that the music industry should quickly develop and implement solutions for the online distribution of music, either in the form of music downloads or customized CDs, and turn them into viable businesses. In the process, they needed to test out new forms of cooperation between the music labels and e-commerce offers in order to provide the customers with unhindered access to a comprehensive music database. At the same time, the music industry needed to develop security and billing systems and quickly agree upon a uniform standard that enabled online distribution while preserving the rights of the artists.

As Middelhoff said, "We need entirely new business models. The music industry should develop offers that are user-friendly, easy to use, comfortable, fast and mobile. The music industry should offer customers the possibility to make an individual selection from a wide repertory and to also decide on flexible billing methods – for example pay-for-play instead of pay-forever. The music industry should take the Internet seriously as an indicator of taste in music and success. The songs being listened to online don't appear on any of the charts. The music industry is faced with tremendous challenges with the advent of the Internet. During the past few decades it has repeatedly understood that it must turn challenges into an opportunity. Let's be brave. If we are, then we can succeed this time."

IS NAPSTER ALREADY DEAD?

It was a healthy sense of reality that propelled Middelhoff, Schmidt and Bertelsmann towards Napster. But did the energetic, upstart pirate of late 1999 and early 2000 really still exist? In the months that followed the announcement in November 2000 and the court ruling against Napster in February 2001, it was clear that Napster was not going to go away easily. There were a number of stories of record companies making court applications to make Napster filter out their songs. These were followed by stories of Napster trying to comply but failing, new court orders to make them try harder and users finding sneaky ways (such as deliberately misspelling artists' names) to get their files registered on the Napster database. For the record companies, trying to kill off Napster has been like trying to kill a multi-headed monster. People still wanted to use Napster software and in reality it has been very hard to stop them.

Nevertheless, there were many inside Napster who, under the weight of lawsuits and general harassment by the rest of the record industry and the media, were beginning to feel burned out. Jordan Ritter, the founding developer of the Napster backend certainly felt rather jaded. "I definitely saw myself as a hacker who regularly formed synergies with music to write code. Napster was a great idea, period – and knowing that I wasn't the only one who felt like that simply helped me understand that Napster was a brilliant idea. Over time, though, I suppose I just grew up. As more lawsuits were filed, as the press began to intensely lambast Napster Inc. for its various and sundry political mistakes, I quickly became jaded, often wondering about our fate as developers and the fate of the revolution. At that point, it became quite difficult to ignore the demand of the market, as well as the demands of those that controlled the market. After the first wild and crazy 6–8 months had passed, Napster became more of a sobering experience for me."

One of the other Napster insiders feels the same way. As time went on, he says, Napster grew so fast that it went out of control because the demands on those who worked there never subsided: "In the beginning, we were all driven by a kind of madness We all eventually burned out, including Shawn Fanning. For a variety of reasons, most significant of which was incompetence in upper management, the backend team never grew to any substantive size. Most people to this day refuse to believe that a team of two or three people run the entire Napster backend, supporting tens of millions of users." Particular wrath is directed at John Fanning, Shawn Fanning's uncle: "John Fanning was Napster's biggest problem," says a second insider.

A third insider talks of his departure: "One of the key reasons I left Napster was that things never slowed down. I was never properly compensated or incentivized to remain working full-tilt for a year straight. The company repeatedly outright refused to publicly recognize or acknowledge my contributions, so, lacking good compensation as well as a general feeling that I was appreciated for the five jobs I did, I resigned. My personal health had deteriorated since I didn't have a great deal of time to keep in shape, and my mental state was not the greatest for lack of a social life … making the decision to leave was not as difficult as some might think."

This insider says, "Outside of adding new features, though, there was still a service to maintain, and that involved many different responsibilities. Napster has always been understaffed and we were all forced to wear many hats. We got a great dose of practical project management and learned all too well the compromise between idealistic engineering and real world business requirements."

At Napster in the early days, the technologists really did lead the company – there were no product plans, there was no real organization or management. Fanning, Ritter and the others would just come up with cool ideas and features, spend a 10 or 20 hour stint coding it up without telling anyone, and then present it to the executive staff. That's how most, if not all of the good that came from Napster came to be. But as Napster's fame spread, so the company's senior management muscled in to get their share of control – and money.

Part of the problem for many of those who worked there in the early days was a sense of acrimony about who would get what portion of the company. Central to these disputes was a sense of injustice felt by the younger technologists at the hands of the older management figures like John Fanning and the CEOs they brought in later. Was there any resentment that the company was controlled by Fanning's family, or that Fanning himself became the icon despite his apparently minimal involvement in both the programming and management of the whole thing? "No comment," says Ritter, "but certainly, contrary to popular belief, none of us except Shawn Fanning have really made any money from Napster."

The third insider adds, "I speak to my friends there quite often though and I'm told that the landscape has changed considerably, that it is a completely different place with a different attitude and mentality. Whether this is a good or bad, I don't really know. What I can say is that Napster used to be a great place to be … now, the culture has completely changed as the company has grown and the original leaders have either left the company or found other things to do."

The second insider goes on, "Napster used to be a great place to be ... we all enjoyed each other's company immensely and lived almost as a family. And those days are now unfortunately well and truly over."

The original spirit that fuelled the Napster boom may have been destroyed, but the force of peer-to-peer distribution was less easy to quell. As we will see in the next chapter, all sorts of other upstarts tried to find a way to get their music online. But would they suffer the same fate as Napster?

NOTES

1   *New York Post*, November 5, 2000.

2   Press release from Bertelsmann AG, October 31, 2000

3   "Let's journey into the digital everyday life of music!" at the Conference at PopKomm in Cologne in August 2000.

CHAPTER 7

Children of Napster – Music and Video

INTRODUCTION

A S EARLIER CHAPTERS HAVE SHOWN, technology could not be ignored once enough people both knew about and actually liked using it. People will embrace file sharing if they want to and there is nothing any other person or organization can do about it. Legal action can slow down or even stop individual companies like Napster but if the technology is freely available and there is a demand for it, it will find a way through to the consumer.

Earlier chapters have looked at the astonishing power of the Napster phenomenon, the growth of the Internet underground and the belated realization by the music industry that powerful forces were at work. Their ultimate reaction in terms of their own ventures into subscription services online are detailed in the next chapter, but in this chapter we focus on the neo-Napsters that sprang up alongside, or in the aftermath of, Napster's popularity. Their fortunes have been decidedly mixed – some have survived, others have been harassed by lawyers of bigger companies, while others still have been shut down by the same.

Even so, there are still hundreds of other organizations more than able to harness the potential of the Napster effect. These are divided broadly into five camps. First, there are those upstarts that are trying to emulate Napster in the area of music and video without falling foul of the law (this chapter). Second, there are those established players that have belatedly recognized the power of the peer-to-peer model and now are reluctantly looking for ways to go with the grain of consumer sentiment – and hopefully gain a profit into the bargain (Chapter 8). Third, there are those who have developed peer-to-peer networks for file sharing (Chapter 9) which, while not commercially-orientated in themselves, have provided a platform for successor versions to make some money. Fourth, there are those who have spotted opportunities not just in file sharing but in wider peer-to-peer developments, such as distributed computing, search engines and even mobile devices (Chapters 10 and 11). Finally, there is the huge commercial potential of digital rights management (Chapter 11), in which companies are making a mint out of preventing the abuse of copyright.

This chapter looks at the first of these groups.

THE CHILDREN OF NAPSTER

Music Crazy

It is impossible in one chapter to go through every Napster alternative in the field of music and video. There are bucket loads of them, with new ones emerging every day. What this chapter does is to steer the reader to the best of the bunch.

In the music arena, as in many other areas of the Internet, making money from peer-to-peer now effectively means charging surfers small download fees for music that is licensed to the provider. There are many others around but upstarts featuring in the field of music and/or video file distribution include Aimster, MP3.com, Flycode (formerly AppleSoup), iMesh.com, Launch Media, OpenCola and Scour. Their fortunes have been decidedly mixed. Scour has been shut down, MP3 has already been bought by Vivendi Universal, while Aimster at the time of writing is involved a messy court battle with AOL Time Warner over its domain name.

Hence, many believe that, despite considerable growing pains, there is money to be made from peer-to-peer. But will the winners be the new upstarts, or the major vendors now spending millions catching up? This chapter looks at the rapid spread of the former.

Aimster

One service developing the Napster model in a new and interesting way is Aimster. Until recently, it had avoided legal problems by offering clients instant messaging services such as AOL's Instant Messenger. This meant that surfers found files by searching the hard drives of their online buddies. Aimster calls this "trading over private exchanges." But at the time of writing, Aimster has just been hit with a lawsuit by the Recording Industry Association of America (RIAA) for copyright infringement. This followed a few days on from an arbitration panel's decision to transfer its domain name to AOL.

Aimster lets its users swap any files stored on their computers with other Aimster users. MP3 music files are the most popular transfers among its users. The system is similar to Napster except that transfers on Aimster are encrypted. Aimster is the brainchild of a group of programmers from Troy, New York. The new service has proved popular and it's easy to see why. The principal benefit of Aimster is that it allows you to search the major file sharing services such as AOL File Sharing, Gnutella (see below) and others – and thereby allows you to target hundreds of thousands of files within seconds. Think of the potential. AOL's Instant Messenger service has an estimated 40–60 million users, with millions of people engaged in file sharing.

What is Aimster trying to be? Johnny Deep, Aimster co-founder, says: "Well I'm hoping that Aimster is going to be one of those pop culture mass market phenomena that just kind of overtakes the world in a heartbeat. We leaked [news of Aimster] to the press ... And there were 100,000 people that have used it in a week. Now if it keeps up like that we might have half a million or a million a month. We might have 10 or 20 million in six months. At which point I would say, that's what I was hoping for."

The reason Aimster has been so popular is that it combines two of the most popular activities on the Internet – file sharing and instant messaging – to provide users with secure file sharing software. The software download relies on AOL's Instant Messenger buddy lists to create groups that can share files through Gnutella's file sharing technology. Gnutella is open-source file sharing technology similar to Napster. Originally developed by AOL's Nullsoft unit, Gnutella now lives on independently.

Until recently it was thought that Aimster would dodge the death by litigation imposed on Napster. It had come under the scrutiny of two powerful forces that have never been shy of going to court to defend their patch in the past: the recording industry (through the Recording Industry Association of America – RIAA) and America Online itself. But unlike Napster, where music files are traded in a public forum, the private exchanges used by Aimster were thought to have fallen on the right side of US law. In the US, consumers can share music for personal use with family and friends – the people who are on their buddy lists, says Johnny Deep.

The *Industry Standard* claimed that Aimster is "the stake in the heart of the record industry."[1] And in the legal sense it is a much harder target for record companies to take a swipe against, although they are trying very hard to do so. From the technological perspective, said Deep at the time, AOL couldn't block Aimster. Others disagree. The *Industry Standard* claimed it would be an easy operation.[2] Just as AOL changed its server-side software to boot users of competing instant-messaging programs off its network, AOL could refuse entry into its closed system to anyone with Aimster installed on their hard disk.

AOL does seem to understand that the surest way to control intellectual property is to control the platform on which that intellectual property is transmitted. The most likely way forward, in spite of the legal action, is that AOL will eventually become involved in the Aimster concept. It could add charges to its network and then charge individuals for use under a whole range of payment schemes, including subscription. And AOL doesn't even have to spend money developing the software, since the nice folks behind Aimster saved it that trouble. Deep feels that the anti-Napster stance taken by Metallica, especially their drummer Lars Ulrich, is mistaken: "Our corporate motto for Aimster is 'Don't put Lars on your buddy list.'"

MP3.com

It seems a strange thing to say about a company that was only incorporated in Delaware in 1998, but MP3.com is already a granddad of the peer-to-peer networking in music. In short, MP3.com is the premier music service provider (MSP) allowing consumers to instantly discover, purchase, listen to, store and organize their music collection from anywhere, at any time, using any Internet device. It is so good at what it does that Vivendi Universal bought it in May 2001 in a deal that valued the company's equity at $372 million.

Michael Robertson, MP3's chairman and chief executive claims that he never intended to incite a rebellion against the music industry. Inadvertently, however, he has. The story began when he founded the Z Company, whose primary focus has been merging search technologies and commerce. As president, he established Filez, the net's largest and fastest file search engine, and Websitez, a domain-name search engine. In November 1997, as he noticed a rise in traffic at sites related to the MP3 digital music format. He bought the lucky domain name MP3.com from a man whose initials were MP. It quickly became one of the leading music destinations on the Internet with half a million unique daily visitors.

Effectively, MP3.com is the centerpiece for the exploding MP3 music movement and works with thousands of artists and hundreds of independent labels to promote and sell their music. Visitors to MP3.com have access to a library of several thousand CD-quality songs. The company's Web site is its focal point. The company allows others to use the Internet and file formats that make music files smaller to enable a growing number of artists to distribute and promote their music to a broad audience and to let consumers access the music catalog. A survey in January 2001 of the MP3.com site revealed that there were 135,1000 approved artists with 862,500 available songs and audio. The site is undoubtedly popular. There was an average of 830,000 daily unique visitors with an incredible 168,000,000 page views per month.

MP3.com has not been without its share of problems. In November, the US courts awarded $53.4 million in statutory damages and attorneys' fees to the Universal Music Group (UMG), the subsidiary of Vivendi Universal, in its copyright infringement suit against MP3.com. The previous January, UMG and others had filed the lawsuit challenging MP3.com's copying of thousands of copyrighted CDs onto its file servers to create its My.MP3.com "locker" service. MP3.com did not appeal against the judgment and MP3's relations with the record companies are relatively good. Zach Horowitz, president and chief operating officer of UMG says, "It was never our intent to put MP3.com out of business with a judgment so large that it would threaten their viability as a company." And it was certainly significant in the light of the subsequent deal with Vivendi Universal that, on completion of the case, UMG granted MP3.com a license for the use of UMG-controlled recordings on the My.MP3.com system.

At the time Michael Robertson said, "We are glad that this case is now behind us and that we will be able to include UMG's music as part of our

My.MP3.com service. We look forward to returning our entire focus to capital-izing on the tremendous opportunity in the digital delivery of music and let-ting consumers listen to CDs which they own in the digital age." Certainly, Robertson and his colleagues are very much at the forefront of carving out the new opportunities: MP3.com has been leading debates on how best to deliver digital music in the wireless world.

Launch Media

Another startup staying close to Napster territory is Launch Media (www.launch.com) which began in August last year. It already has five million members and 250,000 subscribers and focuses on both new and established artists. Yet it has 120,000 songs on its database and many believe that its industry-friendly approach could ensure that it delivers a business model that is both enduring and profitable. Only time will tell.

The Santa Monica firm's portal site offers music news and features cover-ing most major genres, as well as downloadable music, streaming audio and video and community features such as personal home pages, instant messaging and chat rooms. One feature of Launch.com is that it offers music customiza-tion, with LAUNCH.com an intelligent music service that enables members to design their own streaming music station with high quality audio or video. By rating songs, albums, artists and sampling other community members' sta-tions, LAUNCHcast learns to play the types of music individual members want to hear or watch. Another innovation is that it spends its own money producing original tracks.

In many ways Launch Media is starting to look like a radio station, with around half its revenue coming from advertising and sponsorship – $9 million (£6 million) in the first half of 2000. Certainly, the company makes its money through advertising sales, but it also licenses its content to third parties, col-lects fees on music sales and sells its interactive magazine. But don't expect profits any day soon – Launch Media had losses of $37 million (£25 million) in 2000 and advertising revenue, even when driven by ten million page impres-sions a month, is unlikely to make much of a dent on that deficit.

However, many of the smart industry players at the time of writing have faith in Launch Media. Its investors include Intel (6%), NBC (6%) and Sony

Music (5%). In addition, it is engaged in "strategic relationships" with Sony Music, EMI Music, Warner Music Group, Windows Media, NBCi, Intel and Real Networks amid many others. Those at Launch Media believe that it may soon find friends in high places in the political arena. At the start of 2001, CEO Dave Goldberg told *Red Herring* magazine,[3] "Congress is going to get involved this year. There's going to be a tremendous amount of pressure placed on the record labels to be much more proactive by Congress, for two reasons. One, consumers are demanding it and Congress responds to consumers. At a certain point in time, the government will step in and say 'You own these copyrights, but the copyrights are granted to you for the purpose of encouraging you to give people access to them.'"

With its heavyweight backing, Launch Media looks set to be a significant new player in the years ahead. You sense that Goldberg feels rather sorry for the record labels: "The labels are fighting about silly things like if you buy a download, you can't pass that on to someone else, even though if you buy a CD, you can. So we're going to see a lot of fights about these sorts of things. And I think the labels have to be very careful that they're not seen as just being aggressively defensive and not doing stuff proactively. The danger for the labels is that they will get hung out to dry if they're not careful."

Flycode (formerly AppleSoup)

Flycode is, literally, the spawn of Napster. In January 2000, the early Napster founders and investors, Bill Bales and Adrian Scott, took the Napster file sharing ethos one step further forward. They announced the formation of a company known as AppleSoup (now Flycode). The idea was that this was the next generation of peer-to-peer distribution and would allow content owners to distribute "anything digital" via the Internet while giving them a way to control and monetize their intellectual property. Flycode is not targeting music file transfer, however. Instead, it is offering historical and recent video material. "There is a lot of content out there that lots of people want control of – like the highlights from the 1965 World Series. We're talking the universe here," says co-founder Bill Bales.

Flycode is the result of a long friendship in online media. Bales, president and founding CEO, had previously co-founded Quote.com, which was then sold on to Lycos, before investing in and incubating Napster. He served as its VP of business development until December 1999, when he left to co-found Flycode with Adrian Scott. Scott is chairman and VP of engineering. He consulted for Charles Schwab, Hewlett-Packard and Bank of America before becoming an angel investor and advisor to startups. Bales says that Scott was the first person that he phoned for Napster's funding and technological development. "Bill and I had a tremendous experience helping Napster off the ground," says Scott. "We recognized the unstoppable force of peer-to-peer networks. We're not doing music, we're taking peer-to-peer in new directions." Adrian Scott also organizes the Web of Finance, a network of finance and Internet professionals and is something of an internationalist, having studied Cantonese and sales force management at the Chinese University of Hong Kong.

The duo had an unpromising start to their new venture. It was launched as AppleSoup in mid-July 2000. Within a matter of weeks, lawyers for Apple Computer fired off a "cease-and-desist" letter complaining that Web surfers might assume a connection between the computer maker and the startup. In the end, AppleSoup decided to change their name to Flycode. The threats were something of a full circle for Apple. Apple Computer has itself been a victim of the same legal threats back in 1989 when Apple Corps, the Beatles' recording company, sued Apple Computer back for the same reason.

Apple Computer's chagrin may have done Flycode a favor. The dispute usually sets back companies because they need to spend money in re-branding their message. For Flycode, the effect seemed to be to raise public awareness of what the company could offer. And what was on offer was rather enticing. Bales and Scott had spotted that not only were viral networks here to stay, they were largely uncontrollable. The only thing one could do for content owners would be to provide content distribution methods which are more efficient and cost effective, providing a safe way for them to give consumers desktop access to the content they wanted to consume, share and distribute.

When a member requests a specific piece of digital content, Flycode sends him or her directly to another member's hard drive within a matter of seconds to retrieve the file. The platform makes a plethora of specific, valued information available to the masses, without the cumbersome scalability issues of the central server model. Before a copyrighted piece of video is put onto the Flycode network, special software is used to create packaging and assign digital rights. This means it is inaccessible for viewing until the rules and conditions attached to it are met. Access rules are set by the owners of the content and can include conditions such as a limit on the number of people allowed to share it, a time limit on its availability and the collection of user information or payment before a file is allowed to be shown. In the meantime, Flycode's server facilitates contact between users on the network, listing the location of various media files in a central directory, as well as managing the digital rights associated with the content being shared.

For example, User 1 notifies Flycode that he has a secure MPEG video file on his PC. Later, User 2 queries Flycode's directory looking for the same video and is directed to User 1's PC. Flycode ensures that User 2 fulfils the conditions attached to the distribution of the video before being allowed to transfer and then play the video file on his PC.

Flycode includes a layer of software that allows content owners to establish rules about how their materials will be viewed. The company clearly has an eye on video distribution, too. Bales formerly worked for video news Web site On24, and former Home Box Office chairman Frank Biondi owns a 5% share of the company. Critics believe the company has its work cut out signing up content owners that are by and large looking at ways of either forming consortia or going their own way. Skeptics believe that asking them to sign up with a small startup firm is rather like asking Blur to sign with an unknown recording label.

Only time will tell but in November of last year, Flycode edged further forward on the road to respectability. It announced the appointment of a media and entertainment heavyweight, Mark Rudolph, as its chief executive officer. Rudolph was most notably a pioneer of CNN's international division, leading its expansion into a widely distributed and profitable international satellite channel. Rudolph has a great track record. He most recently served as deputy chief executive officer for FilmFour in the UK. Meanwhile, Bill Bales is continuing on the executive team as vice-president of business development.

iMesh

With the RIAA finally having succeeded in shutting down Napster, iMesh is likely to be among the beneficiaries. Created by programmers in Israel, it is similar to Napster in its file sharing approach. It has an excellent program that lets you search for and share multimedia files easily and reliably. Its most obvious use comes from the illicit sharing and downloading of MP3s. But unlike Napster, it can also be used to share video and image files.

The company was founded in 1999 and has quickly made inroads into the file sharing market with its free revolutionary application for searching the Internet. Its technology allows users to access and share information directly from one desktop to another, rather than through servers. And unlike Napster, iMesh has always been very concerned to protect itself from legal action by stating its efforts to achieve a legal file sharing environment through the Internet.

Mad about movies

DivX

If the movie industry ever felt slightly smug watching the sufferings of their recording industry brethren, then those days are now long gone. The movie industry has been watching the legal battles involving Napster with some interest for some time. But industry groups such as the Motion Picture Association of America (MPAA) seemed pretty sure that widespread piracy of movies was years away. Surely the movie industry would learn from the anarchy taking over the world of music.

That was before DivX turned up. DivX is a file format (not related to the failed technology of the same name pioneered by the company Circuit City a couple of years back) that allows the copying of entire DVD discs with little loss of quality. The information on the DVD can be compressed into about 600 MB, between 10% and 20% of the size of the original DVD. This means that those who use the Internet with fast lines such as cable modems or DSL can download entire movies in one or two hours. Better still, they can play them with the fullest stereo sound and full screen video. The downloaded movie can be burned onto a CD with a CD recorder, or stored on a computer hard drive.

Until recently it hasn't been practical for a normal computer user to download a movie. While the attractions of MP3 files for sound files are well known and manageable through relatively slow modems, film files are often enormous, taking many hours or days to download and huge hard drives on which to keep them. Even then, the quality of the visuals and sound are usually poor.

DivX is different. What makes it possible are two pieces of software: the first is an application that cracks the encryption on DVDs, the secret encoding that is supposed to prevent their being copied to a PC in the first place. The second is a component of Microsoft's Windows Media Player that compresses digital files.

The two pieces of software were linked together by a Californian-based Frenchman, Jerome Rota. He used the name of DivX as a joke. It was deliberately designed to make fun of Circuit City's alternative DVD technology that was marketed based on its anti-copying feature, but failed. Although Microsoft had, at the time of writing, threatened to take action against DivX, Monsieur Rota has been working on a completely legal implementation of the DivX theme that won't use Microsoft technology at all. He has, in the process, worked with others to open a company that pursues digital video. This is known as ProjectMayo.com, which, along with another known as 3ivx.com, is a new version of the compression technology that doesn't use Microsoft technology. Rota runs ProjectMayo.com and 3ivx.com in an open source manner (i.e. it is developed by many programmers working together with the finished project belonging to them all collectively). This will make files even smaller, make pictures and sound of better quality and provide streaming movies. Streaming means playing them as they're downloaded so there's no need to wait to see the movie.

The site is unquestionably popular. Daniel Marlin runs the MyDivX.com Web site, which tells visitors everything they need to know about the new format. He claims that in six weeks over the summer of 2000, the Internet underground community went from not knowing about it to over 100,000 hits per day. The site is scrupulously careful about treading the line between obeying the law and busting it wide open. It has the software to play movies but no actual movies. To do that it would have to look at file swapping networks such as Scour, Gnutella and Freenet. Scour has been sued by the MPAA, but most of the other DivX sites seem to be operating perfectly legally.

The movie industry's relatively relaxed attitude is exemplified by Hemanshu Nigam, director of world-wide Internet enforcement for the MPAA. "When you use it legally," he told the MyDivX.com Web site in February 2001, "DivX isn't a threat. It's how you use the compression software. When you use it legally, the technology is a nice piece of work. When you use it illegally you are interfering with our copyright." The MPAA in 2000 sent out 2000 "cease-and-desist" letters, a figure that he expects to "increase exponentially" in 2001: "We're sending out letters to people who are distributing movies that are compressed using DivX and that number has been increasing steadily. We're not trying to put the technology back in the bag: that doesn't make any sense. What we're saying is the technology is out there and if you use it incorrectly we'll try to stop you."

Chief executive of the Motion Picture Association of America, Jack Valenti claims that his industry will not refute technology in the way that the recording industry has. In July 2000 he told the *New York Daily News*, "We're not against new technology. We're against new technology used illegitimately. And DivX is a compression technology. There's nothing illegal about the technology. It just makes it quicker to bring [a movie] down." That said, the copyright issue has engulfed the movie industry much more quickly than anyone had anticipated. Many in the industry thought that it would take widespread use of broadband for movie copying technology to take hold. Very few thought that someone would come up with a way to cut the size of movie files.

Scour

While DivX has played things by the book, others have not been so lucky. The Scour Web site at the start of 2001 said simply that "Centerspan Communications has won control of Scour's assets, including its award-winning media search engine and peer-to-peer file exchange. Centerspan plans to re-launch Scour as a secure and legal distribution channel for music, movies, e-books, images and documents." Therein lies a tale.

Centerspan Communications purchased Scour's assets after Scour filed for protection under Chapter 11 of the Bankruptcy Code in October 2000. Centerspan Communications Corp describes itself as "a developer and marketer of peer-to-peer Internet communication and collaboration solutions." The new Scour was due to be launched in the first quarter of 2001.

Scour shut down the Scour Exchange in November 2000 under the weight of legal action. Until then it had been a broadband entertainment portal on the Internet and a very useful one too. The site helped its users find almost every kind of music including streaming radio stations, movies and videos from all over the Web. Basically, Scour's focus on multimedia made it different from any other guide or search engine on the Internet.

The Scour directory was powerful. It could find online and broadcast radio stations from around the globe, sports audio and video clips, music videos and "behind the scenes" mini-documentaries, full-length movies and even animated shows. It was divided into four content categories: music zone; radio zone; movie zone and tools zone. Each zone had pages containing daily multimedia recommendations, news and a more detailed breakdown to narrow your search. Scour also offered exclusive technologies to make the most of multimedia Internet destinations.

Dan Rodriguez, the president of Scour before legal clouds surrounded it, denied that that Scour was another Napster. Scour, he claimed, began two years earlier as a college project, as a search engine – and nothing more: "We were on broadband connections in the dorm rooms in UCLA, and once our Web pages moved a little bit faster what did we want to do online? Typically, we wanted digital music and multimedia content. So we built a search engine to find that." Rodriguez claims that Scour had the goal of creating a business model that serves copyright holders as well as consumers.

Even so, trying to balance these two forces was easier said than done. Rodriguez told *Salon.com* that the hostility to his Scour venture came as something of a surprise. Certainly the company had taken a different approach to Napster. Scour had consulted from the beginning with intellectual property experts to ensure that its network was not breaching the Digital Millennium Copyright Act, the federal law governing online copyright liability for Internet service providers and search tools. Rodriguez said, "We had 27 plaintiffs in the lawsuit against us, so that was obviously a ball that got rolling before we were served. But from our perspective it was a surprise. We came with a fundamentally different philosophy to these guys and we said we really want to work out a business solution because there's this huge consumer demand here that it only makes sense to harness. That was our intention and we would have preferred to sit down and work out a business relationship and work out a business strategy. But litigation was their approach – we just hope it is part of the negotiation process."

Well, as we know now, it wasn't. Scour.com was sued in July 2000 by the Recording Industry Association of America (RIAA), the Motion Picture Association of America and the National Music Publishers Association. The suit alleged that a service run by the company, Scour Exchange, contributed to copyright infringement by letting people trade music, video and other files. The case, despite what Rodriguez said, did bear strong parallels to the suit brought by the RIAA against Napster.

But at least everyone now knows the name of Scour.com. User numbers increased substantially, particularly after the Napster hearing. As Rodriguez said, "Well, from before the lawsuit to a week after, we grew our user base by 100%. Currently [in August] there are about 70,000 users online sharing almost 5 million files at any given time. We've had about 2.5 million downloads of the application." You could argue that all publicity is good publicity when it comes to making a name on the underground Internet. Centerspan Communications could have a winning brand on its hands when Scour's re-launched (legal) service gets underway.

NOTES

1   *Industry Standard*, December 11, 2000.

2   *Industry Standard*, December 11, 2000.

3   *Red Herring*, January 2, 2001.

CHAPTER 8

Post-Napster: Will Online Subscription Prosper?

INTRODUCTION

I N THE EARLY MONTHS OF 2001, in the aftermath of the Napster ruling, the major record labels made a series of announcements. These announcements made it easier to understand why most of them had refused point blank to collaborate with Napster. "People have often thought that an alliance with Napster is the only solution, but I don't see why we should give the advantage to pirates," said Vivendi boss Jean-Marie Messier.

After having taken Napster to the cleaners, the major record labels went about creating their own online subscription offerings. Bertelsmann carefully hedged their bets by also taking part in some of these new ventures.

THE MAJOR RECORD LABELS DIP THEIR TOES

There were two new ventures of particular significance. One was MusicNet, which comprised three of the world's largest record labels and the Internet media software company RealNetworks. The three majors to take part in the project were AOL Time Warner, which owned the Warner Music Group, EMI Group and Bertelsmann Music Group. These three, together with RealNetworks, got together to build a subscription service which would then be licensed to other online music services. MusicNet plans to offer the technology and services that allow online music companies to provide downloads and "streaming" of music over the Internet for a subscription fee and testing of the service was due to start in the fall of 2001. All three majors were equity shareholders in the new venture but RealNetworks was the largest single stakeholder with a 40% stake in the new company.

The other major venture is Duet, the creation of the other two labels: Vivendi Universal, the owner of Universal Music, which in February 2001 announced a long-rumored partnership with Sony to create a rival online music service to Napster. Duet was expected to provide access to the entire catalogs of both companies, bringing together Universal acts from Eminem to Texas with Sony artists like Jennifer Lopez and The Manic Street Preachers. The end result would bring together half the world's music.

The Duet venture received significant backing from online search engine Yahoo! Yahoo! at one point had derived 80% of its money from the cyclical advertising market and had been looking for ways of earning more revenue from regular subscribers. The idea was that Yahoo! would market Duet's online subscription service to its nearly 200 million users.

These two ventures raise the possibility of a "celestial jukebox" system featuring all the planet's favorite tracks – if the two projects could find some way of getting together. Vivendi Universal boss Messier says that it will be possible to license the Duet platform to other record companies: "We hope others will join us … We are open to AOL-Time Warner or EMI or even Bertelsmann Music Group." Indeed, he says, "We are not even closing the door to Napster … but they have to get back on track in terms of respecting copyright."

At the moment, the major record labels' efforts bear little resemblance to file sharing as millions of Napster users came to know it. Both these ventures are subscription services where the record companies retain a large element of control. This is file sharing writ small, although Duet's subscription service will let users compile personal play lists and share them with other Duet members.

MAJORS AND THE MINORS

There are also plenty of other ventures between the major record companies and the minor legal music services to be found on the Internet. Aside from the deal between Bertelsmann and Napster, there are now many others and what follows represents just the highlights.

Sometimes they take the form of acquisitions. For example, Universal Music Group agreed to acquire digital music retailer Emusic. Emusic sells

MP3 tracks and albums from 700 independent labels and would give Duet, of which UMG is a part, a proven platform for selling downloadable music by track, by album and by monthly subscription. UMG's purchase of Emusic would also provide Duet with exclusive digital distribution deals with the independent labels.

Then there are deals in which several of the majors have licensed their products, with EMI being at the forefront of many deals (see box overleaf). On top of these, TouchTunes Music entered a five year licensing deal with Sony Music Publishing, which gives TouchTunes the right to copy, download and play the Sony Music Publishing repertoire on its jukeboxes. Meanwhile, BMG Entertainment, Universal Music Group, Warner Music Group and Sony Music Entertainment have all licensed their catalogs for use in Click Radio's interactive music services. ClickRadio's service lets users customize music play lists from their computer hard drives.

Eric Sheirer, an analyst at Forrester Research sees all such deals as the start of the legitimate development of the music industry online: "These announcements – all coming as a flurry on top of each other – legitimate the thought that the digital music market is taking shape in a fairly healthy way versus a single label service. The prospect that we see, in a year or two, is that of many different music services innovating and out-competing each other, and that's a great music opportunity."

SUBSCRIPTIONS AND DOWNLOADS

Several reports published in 2000 and 2001 suggested that much of the growth in the music industry would be fuelled by online subscription services. Jupiter MMXI predicts that subscription services will account for almost twice that of digital downloads in 2005. Have the researchers got it right?

It is important to understand the differences between online subscription and allowing downloading of individual files. Digital downloads offer the possibility of changes in the relationships between the various parties – artist, record company, distributor and retailer – in the chain between the creation of the product and the consumer. They also allow the possibility that the artist could form a direct relationship with the consumer of their product. Even so,

SOME OF EMI'S NEW MEDIA DEALS

All of the major record labels have started to do licensing deals with online companies. Here are some of the deals that EMI has managed to put together.

Musicmaker.com

A limited, exclusive license agreement with Musicmaker for custom compilation CDs. Customers accessing the musicmaker.com Web site can select tracks from different artists and create their own custom compilations, which are manufactured in CD format and shipped to them.

Listen.com

EMI have made an investment in Listen.com. Listen.com's Internet music download directory helps users find music on the Net that has been digitized through various technologies including Liquid Audio.

BT Cellnet

There is also an exclusive deal between EMI and BT Cellnet's Genie Internet partners to deliver the latest news from the world of pop music direct to the UK's 20 million mobile phone users. Customers can access the Genie Internet portal where they will be able to get exclusive news headlines on EMI artists delivered direct to their mobile phone from the Internet via free SMS text messages.

Hithive.com

EMI Group has agreed to license a major portion of its recording catalog to HitHive, a company that is developing services to deliver digital music to cellular phones and other consumer devices. HitHive's technology is designed to allow consumers to invite up to 25 friends to listen to the suggested recordings for a limited time, but prevents users from distributing other copies.

Musicbank.com

Musicbank, an online music company, has reached an agreement with EMI Group to license its recordings. The service also allows consumers who own

CDs to be able to listen to them online using Musicbank's digital-music service without having to upload the recordings manually. Musicbank plans to offer its service later through cable television systems to homes and through wireless providers to consumers' cars. The company also plans to offer a subscription-based service and a legal file sharing service similar to Napster.

a download is still essentially a download, selected and offered for sale by a record company to the consumer.

This is a very different kettle of fish from subscription services. If online subscription proves viable, it means a big shift in business plans for the major record labels. These allow the consumer a sort of "all you can eat" guide. – a wide choice of music for a fixed fee rather than the usual sale of individual items at individual prices. On the face of it, a fixed fee should be attractive to the record companies: it gives them a predictable regular income while consumers get a wide choice of music.

According to surveys published in *Music & Copyright* magazine, subscription services will become the fastest growing element with the expanding online market, accounting for a predicted 18% (or $890m) of total online sales of $5.4 billion and for 4.5% of total sales of $21.6 billion by 2005. Jupiter forecasts that in 2005, subscription sales will represent almost twice the value of digital downloads ($531m) and almost twice the percentage of digital downloads (2.5%) as a percentage of the total retail value of the US market. These figures preceded the downturn in the US economy from late 2000 onwards and so probably overestimate the speed at which the online market will grow, but they reveal important shifts in music consumption patterns which will take place in the next four years. Jupiter's predictions assume online sales will add to traditional sales from stores rather than substitute them.

An important point is that pretty soon the digital technology that supports online sales will become much more widespread. By 2005 there will be over 50 million optical storage devices that will be compatible with portable digital music devices, and broadband access will be available in 36% of US online households. It is thought that this could benefit subscriptions rather than downloads. With digital downloading, payment is required every time a download is made and there are of course security issues involved with downloading that do not exist with respect to a subscription service.

Other research by Jupiter is interesting. Jupiter asked users to rate a series of features of a subscription service on a scale of 1 to 5. Users rated guaranteed file quality and the certainty that a file will be virus protected at an average of 3.8, the highest in the survey. Even so, 20% of respondents said they would be willing to accept a number of constraints on downloading from a subscription service. These included limited copies (27%) having to see adverts as part of the process (24%) a need to register (23%) and having to download specific software (21%). However, at the same time only 5% of interviewees said they would sign up to a fee-paying subscription service if it meant they could only use the downloaded file on a limited number of devices. Similarly, 7% thought that the timing-out of a file – where it expires after a set period – was unacceptable, while 10% considered tracking of their usage of files – a very important issue for record companies – also unacceptable.

HAVE THE MAJORS GOT IT ALL WRONG?

There may well be an outpouring of services online but will the major record labels really benefit from the demand for online music? The majors have realized that they need to get online, but there are question marks over whether they have gone about it in the right way.

Many experts think that they haven't. The biggest issue is that of price. The worry is that the majors think that people will be willing to pay the same sort of prices online for MP3s that they pay for CDs. The evidence is, overwhelmingly, that they will not.

While not all music lovers are freeloaders, they are not exactly mugs either. The price of CDs in shops cannot be appealing if one knows that the music is readily available free of charge over the Internet. Edward Skira, project consultant for Canadian research company, In the Name of Cool, sums it all up nicely: "The music industry has to wake up and recognize that that the one-hit, 15-song CD isn't working anymore. The music buyer wants choice and if the industry doesn't provide that choice, they'll explore the option that technology provides."

Chuck D, co-founder of rappers Public Enemy, is a highly vocal critic of the major record labels, particularly on the issue of price and value. The trouble, he says, is that the majors simply don't understand the idea that people just don't want to buy an entire album online – and certainly not at the same prices that they could get the album in the store: "Can you believe it? EMI started selling albums online at $17.99 because they see it as just another way to get money out of the consumer. This isn't like CD taking over from vinyl, when my Uncle Pete went out and replaced his entire [vinyl] record collection because the record companies were going to heavy on CDs. Now you don't need to buy a whole album. People want what people want, but are people going to pay $17.99 for an online album? No way!"

IT EITHER HAS TO BE WIDE ENOUGH ...

Whether the subscription model really works is doubtful, unless the offering is wide enough. None of the subscription services available to consumers are wide ranging enough to attract the mainstream market. MP3.com's classic channel offers under 4000 tracks and Emusic offers only 120,000 tracks. These channels have also been losing out to Napster which of course was free. Shawn Conahan, vice-president and head of MP3 mobile, MP3.com, says the difficulties in making a service comprehensive has much to do with the slowness with which the major record labels deal with copyright issues: "The process itself of securing rights to stream music makes it really difficult to get our sort of service off the ground. We can't just get the major labels to help us work out who owns what" Is this through incompetence or a more cynical approach by the majors? "It's really difficult to say," says Conahan, "but more likely to be the former. Even so, there's an unbelievable morass of hands reaching into the pie." Chris Cass, managing director of online music provider Vitaminic, agrees that the majors have been very slow in taking music online "but you can understand why from their perspective. Fortunately, for the whole industry, their consumers forced them to do it."

Conahan says that even the major labels' online catalogs couldn't go any-where near keeping the consumer happy, hence the attempt of the majors to disguise their services under brand names like MusicNet and Duet: "The big problem for the record labels is that no one ever says, 'I'm a Warner Broth-ers fan.' I wouldn't pay for a site only run by Universal-Vivendi. I certainly wouldn't know on which label my favorite artist is recording their work. And why on earth should I want to know? I just want to go to a site which has all my favorite artists."

... OR DEEP ENOUGH

Ultimately the majors realize that you have to be offering one of two things online. Either you give a wide range of content, or you offer specialized con-tent in one area. Majors on their own can do neither. Chuck D agrees with this point: "One of the most important things is that it's OK to be some kind of super site but in the niche markets you have to be focused on what you're doing. If you don't focus on what you're doing there is really no point in offer-ing anything."

This is something well understood by Gavin Robertson, managing direc-tor of Musicindie, which represents the independent record labels. He claims that one of the key problems in the music industry is that music is seen as some sort of generic quality: "If all music was the same then why buy some and not other types of music? People buy different things because they have different tastes and styles. People want music in different forms not just one form. That's the whole point." Shawn Cohahan says, "Even if there was a country music store with every single country record ever made in it, I would still walk on by. But those who love country music will be demanding that degree of specializa-tion in online music and the major record labels are not yet able to organize themselves to that sort of thing."

WILL PEOPLE PAY FOR A "SUBSCRIPTION" NAPSTER?

With the online music market developing so rapidly, Napster's impact on its development is undoubted. But the question remains as to whether it still has relevance in its own right or whether it was merely the catalyst for a revolution. At the heart of this debate is the question of whether people would be prepared to pay for a Bertelsmann-Napster subscription scheme.

Napster users have been greater purchasers of music than non-Napster users. But research from Jupiter shows that the 18 to 24 year old group spends less than $20 a month on music. Anecdotal evidence also suggests that during the early growth of Napster, CD album sales had declined in shops close to colleges in the US – much early Napster use was through high-bandwidth college Internet links. Even so, the fact that students are not universally hostile to paying small fees for downloads is borne out by a recent survey by US-based digital entertainment research firm Webnoize. It found that out of 4300 college students, 58% said they would be willing to pay as much as $15 per month to use the service.

Most of the other Napster users say that, hypothetically, they would join a fee-paying subscription service should it be made available. But Simon Scott, a vice-president at Intertrust, the digital rights management (DRM) solutions provider is another one who is wary about the differences between what people say and what people do. He says that people don't actually have the motivations they claim when it comes to questions of subscription. "If you said to people you can buy this encrypted CD for your own use for only $5 or you can buy the same CD for $10 for sharing with your friends then that would be a more revealing question. It's a better question than whether you would pay to get MP3s through the Internet."

The evidence so far suggests that, as the availability of music has been curtailed by filtering and the specter of subscription has risen, users have, in fact, fled the Napster service. A piece of research from the beginning of May 2001 from online music specialist Webnoize claims that the number of songs being downloaded via Napster has dropped by more than a third. The figures were the first full month's statistics since the court injunction that ruled Napster introduced a music-blocking technology on its service.

According to Webnoize, Napster users in April downloaded 1.6 billion songs which was down by 36% from 2.5 billion in March and 43% down from the February peak of 2.8 billion. Even more interesting was the fall in the number of songs available for download per user to 37 files in April compared to

74 files in March and 220 files at its peak at the beginning of February. Feelings are mixed on whether Napster will make a comeback as a subscription service. In spite of its problems, millions of songs are still being downloaded from Napster because it is simple to use, very good at what it does and very useful. Even so, it does throw a question mark over Bertelsmann's ability to build a legal, subscription-based version of Napster.

Bertelsmann's Andreas Schmidt believes that the economic argument will win the day and that that doesn't depend on winning over all of Napster's existing users. He believes that Napster's subscription service will succeed even if only 30% of Napster's users agree to pay up. Adam Powell, CEO of Angry Coffee, which offers a free meta-search engine offering much of the same functionality as Napster, told *Broadband Week* magazine, "70% of the air traffic (will migrate to) using free sites."[1] Even so, Powell and others think that with or without Napster, subscription services will become a mainstream way of consuming music within three years, particularly as broadband networks make online music more mainstream.

Gavin Robertson is one of those who thinks that the move towards a subscription model was as likely as night following day: "For Napster to survive alone would have meant that it had found some kind of business model, but all they had, for all of their popularity, was an illegal free music service. They were never going to make a long-term business out of it." Now it has been looking for a way forward that gives it a legal long-term business model. "But to be brutally honest," says Robertson, "the only way that its legal service can survive is when they offer something that illegal ones cannot. And yet with all the filtering that Napster has been ordered to undertake by the courts, Napster's legal service is not even as good as it used to be."

HOW CAN ANYONE COMPETE WITH "FREE?"

Mark Hardie, chief executive officer of ETC Music Inc and former digital music analyst with Forrester Research says that the Bertelsmann-Napster deal was intriguing, but risky: "They're staking their claim that on the other side of all the legal action there will still be a Napster and the question is whether or not Napster the brand is of value, and they're arguing it is." But will Napster's community move with it? "It's going to be interesting to see how you convert Napster into a subscription model because I think it's appeal is that it is free," he said. "Napster under a payment model or Napster with a subscription fee isn't Napster, it's something else."

In the end, the distinction between a free service and a subscription service is less financial and more psychological. Many of the later older adopters of Napster can easily afford to pay for a subscription service whether it be from Napster or from any other subscription service. The difference is far more psychological. Having to pay squelches that kid in a toy shop feeling. Psychologists say that Americans and to a certain extent the rest of the world, are clearly becoming addicted to the idea of free music and contemptuous of the idea of intellectual property in general.

Psychologist Peter Kollock is pessimistic about the viability of a Napster-like subscription music service. And there is good reason to believe that people are having trouble wrapping their heads around the idea that intellectual property is as sacrosanct as "real" property: "Certainly there are no easy answers for the record industry. An affordable subscription service as easy to use as Napster may not make any money. People's expectations have changed too much. They are treating music swapping as though it's a right ... it's going to be hard to get this genie back in the bottle."

IT'S NOT WHAT YOU SELL BUT HOW YOU SELL IT

Sometimes it's not what you sell but how you sell it. Chris Cass, of Vitaminic, says that one answer to the question "Why should I pay $5.95 per month?" is to not sell subscriptions directly to consumers at all. "You don't have to sell directly to the consumer. You can bundle it up with other marketing. For instance, you can open an online bank account with music given away free online." What is difficult says Cass, is that it is very difficult to sell when someone else is giving the stuff away free. "It's very difficult indeed to sell beer in a free bar. What record companies need is a multi-channel distribution process."

Then there's the question of cutting out the bureaucracy and paperwork. Gavin Robertson, managing director of Musicindie says that consumers don't really want to subscribe but not because they object to paying for content: "It's simply that people don't want to enter into a contract online to subscribe or download music." The important thing, adds John Esner, a partner at digital music specialist solicitors Olswang, is to remember who is doing the bulk of music buying in this business: "It's the kids. They will continue to be the driving force from the market. They ask their parents for the money for music. They love text messaging because there are no contracts and all that sort of thing involved. That's the way forward." Simon Scott, vice-president at Intertrust, adds that his company is developing ways of making this happen directly by allowing people to make cash purchases through the Internet.

Then there is the whole new area of distribution to devices other than PCs. This subject alone could take up a whole book. Gavin Robertson has the final say: "The debate is in its infancy for as long as we're talking about peer-to-peer file sharing delivered through the PC. Real peer-to-peer is all about gadgets talking to each other, not PC users. One of the first killer applications will be files delivered to the car while you're getting from A to B."

CONCLUSION

As far as the offerings of music online are concerned, ultimately some sort of business model will emerge in which the issues of intellectual property and file sharing will be able to live comfortably with one another. Why? Because it has to, says Curtis Robert, the CEO of DMOD (Digital Music on Demand), based in Boston: "Intellectual property issues and file sharing issues will find a way through this. I say this simply because the technology exists. And because the technology exists, the problems won't go away. And because the problems won't go away, there can and there must be a solution."

Robert is probably right. There can and must be solutions in this area. But the issue of peer-to-peer services as the major record labels perceive it is a far cry from a brave new world of mass peer-to-peer file sharing via a variety of devices alluded to above by the likes of Gavin Robertson. And that in turn is a country mile from the potential of peer-to-peer networking that is so intriguing to much of the business community. The terms Napster, file sharing and peer-to-peer have crystallized the debate for all, but still mean different things to many. Definitions are used loosely and interchangeably in a way that often clouds possible answers to the debate.

So, at the center of the debate is continuing confusion over what we really mean by peer-to-peer networking. The next chapter tries to clarify this issue because only by making this clarification can one truly understand the true business legacy of the Napster phenomenon.

NOTE

1   *Broadband Week*, December 2000.

CHAPTER 9

Napster, File Sharing and Peer-to-Peer – the Impact on the Wider Business World

INTRODUCTION

THIS CHAPTER LOOKS AT how the success of Napster relates to the wider debate about the potential of peer-to-peer networking. They are not the same thing. The problem with any new development or trend is that people start to define it in terms of a buzzword or phrase. Pretty soon they start to apply it to too many things and, worse, the wrong things. Such is the case with peer-to-peer.

The trouble with the label peer-to-peer is that it hasn't really helped anybody understand what it means. You would think that the definition of peer-to-peer was obvious: it's people or things communicating with each other. Servers talking to each other are peer-to-peer and in one sense, making and receiving telephone calls are as well. Yet Napster is, in the strict sense of the word, not peer-to-peer because it uses a centralized server to do its work in compiling lists of available files.

Sometimes it is not such a good idea to take everything too strictly. Talking on the telephone may be peer-to-peer but so what? We know it's peer-to-peer and we do it already. But to broaden a definition to include Napster means that we can at least make some attempt to explain the irresistible forces underlying the Napster phenomenon – something which a lot of people, especially the major record labels, are really struggling to understand.

WHAT PEER-TO-PEER REALLY MEANS

For many years computers have been "peering" with each other through e-mail and other means, so to this extent, the architecture of peer-to-peer computing is nothing new at all. What is new is that those points that constitute peer-to-peer systems, the PCs connected to the Internet, move from being at the outer reaches of the Internet system – essentially just the receivers of information accessed from servers – to having significant or even total autonomy from central servers. Effectively, the common thing holding all peer-to-peer applications together is that they are systems that make better use of these resources at the edge of the Internet, be it storage space, content or human presence. And by definition, getting access to such decentralized resources has to mean that applications need to be developed that can work with lots of users coming and going of their own free will.

Perhaps then, the way of defining peer-to-peer in a more useful manner is to ask firstly whether it gives the devices or people at the edge of the network a real level of autonomy. The second question is whether it is flexible enough to allow the resources they hold to connect with one another in a highly unstable and rapidly changing environment. Napster can live comfortably within this two-pronged definition.

Most companies from the old and new economies can clearly point to the assets that make their company work. But Napster's asset (the software program that makes it all work) can be found on tens of millions of PCs across the world. This asset is both giving autonomy to those people and allowing as few or as many of them to communicate with each other for as long or as short a period of time as they wish.

Put a little more technically, Napster comes into the peer-to-peer definition because Napster users bypass the domain naming system (DNS) that people associated with the Internet. Once the Internet protocol addresses of the song you want to upload have been identified, control of the file transfers to the PC rather than to any central server. E-mail, however, would not be a peer-to-peer network under this definition because your address is still dependent on a machine. If you change your Internet service provider (ISP), your old e-mail address disappears because it is linked to the DNS's machine-centered perspective on the Internet.

NAPSTER IS KEY TO PEER-TO-PEER BECAUSE NAPSTER WORKS

Napster's use of a central filing system notwithstanding, a wider definition of peer-to-peer has to be made quite simply because it is too big to ignore. Whatever happens to Napster in the long term, the reality is that it has proved itself to be an outstanding example of the success of the peer-to-peer revolution. It is already a mainstream phenomenon, with an adoption rate outstripping even the likes of Hotmail and ICQ, the first PC-based chat system. Whether the definition works for you or not, the fact remains that people use Napster.

The first point to remember about Napster is that it was written to cure a specific problem. One of Fanning's college roommates was obsessively interested in MP3s and music Internet sites, but complained that many of the links on sites often led nowhere and indices were often out of date. The technological solutions found were designed to focus on the needs of people, like his roommate, who requested them. People wanted something like Napster, so Fanning did his best to come up with the goods.

TO DECENTRALIZE OR NOT?

In responding to a demand, Napster highlights much of the problem, not just with peer-to-peer models, but with the introduction of new technology more generally. Many people talk about decentralization and successful peer-to-peer applications in the same breath, as if the only criterion for the success of the latter is to set up a system that incorporates the former. Yet decentralization does not provide copper-bottomed guarantees of peer-to-peer utopia.

Indeed, Clay Shirky, a partner for technology and product strategy at the Accelerator Group, which invests active strategic capital in digital businesses, points out that very often some degree of centralization is necessary to make many systems work. Most search engines, he points out in Andy Oram's excellent book *Peer-to-Peer*, work best when they can search a central database rather than launch a search of peers. Electronic marketplaces need to aggregate supply and demand in a single place at a single time in order to arrive at a single price. Says Shirky,[1] "Any system that requires real-time group access or rapid searches through large sets of unique data will benefit from centralization in ways that will be difficult to duplicate in peer-to-peer systems. The genius of Napster is that it understands and works within these limitations. Napster mixes centralization and decentralization beautifully."

The centralization end of Napster builds up the list of songs available through users and, because the actual content is on millions of computers around the world, the chances of finding a particular song are high, even if the chances of any particular user being online at the time are low. In doing so, Napster has the strength of a central list and the ease of decentralized storage. In effect, its inability to fall within a strict definition of peer-to-peer is a strength, not a weakness, in its success story.

Nevertheless, it is the decentralized storage of files on the PCs of Napster's millions of users that is leveraging a whole new area of untapped power and this process is helped by the move to greater bandwidth. This allows PCs the ability to act as a server from their disk space as well as download from elsewhere. It is the ability of Napster to harness the power of the PC, until recently the far-flung outpost of the Internet empire that has created a lot of interest in all manner of peer-to-peer models. Their common feature is that they all try to harness this power.

THE FREE SPIRITS OF DECENTRALIZATION

It is worth looking at a few examples of truly decentralized peer-to-peer systems. There are some file sharing methods that are not owned by anyone in particular. While this makes it hard for anyone to make money from these systems, they do point the way to the commercial potential of other systems, which will be discussed in next two chapters.

Gnutella

In many people's eyes, Gnutella is a sort of Napster-lite. It's legal, so it makes you feel better about using it (that is if you felt bad about using Napster in the first place) but most people say that it is less effective. Nevertheless, it has become the first large scale, fully decentralized system running on the public Internet. Unlike Napster, it does not rely on any sort of central authority to organize the network or to broker transactions. All you need is to connect to one host.

One important thing to say is that there is no official program called Gnutella. The original program was released as a test program. What it is today is an open, decentralized peer-to-peer search system that is mainly used to find files. Just like Freenet (see below), Gnutella is neither a company, nor an application nor a Web site. It is instead the name for a language of communication, and any software that speaks the language is Gnutella-compatible.

In spite of its completely decentralized nature, it is possible to trace the founding fathers of Gnutella. It was conceived and developed by Justin Frankel and Tom Pepper at Nullsoft in March 2000. These two were part of an independent group interested in the idea of peer-to-peer technology. To use Gnutella you need what is known as a "servant" application. This allows you to search for, download and upload any type of file. Because the Gnutella protocol is open there are many interoperable servants to choose from. And with a servant you can either form a private network or you can connect to the general public network. Some servants are open source, but contrary to popular misconception, the original is not. By way of contrast, Gnutella is far more flexible.

The key point to remember is that Gnutella puts personal contact back into the Internet. When you run Gnutella software, you bring with you information that you want to make public. That could be nothing or it could be one file or your entire hard disk. Effectively the software is a mini-search engine and a file serving system rolled into one. When you search the Gnutella network, the search is transmitted to everyone in your Gnutella network "horizon."

On the downside for Gnutella is that if no one in particular controls its development it becomes harder to gauge its improvements. Complaints of slow downloads and relatively complicated sign up procedures have dampened enthusiasm for Gnutella, which is still waiting for major fixes. Complicating the protocol's development is the fact that it has branched down several different paths. Gnutella has also had problems with dramatic slowdowns in responsiveness and many users have reported serious instabilities in the network.

This will always be a major problem for peer-to-peer networks such as Gnutella and Freenet, which have no central authority. Rob Johnson, an open-

THE DIFFERENCE BETWEEN NAPSTER AND GNUTELLA

Gene Kan of Gnutella highlights the difference between using Gnutella and Napster in terms of a cocktail party:

Gnutella cocktail party

1 You enter at the foyer and say hello to the closest person.

2 Shortly your friends see you and come to say hello.

3 You would like to find the tray of sushi, so you ask your nearby friends. None of your drunken friends know where the sushi is, but they ask the people standing nearby. Those people in turn ask the people near them, until the request makes its way around the room.

4 Partygoers on the other side of the room have the tray. They pass back the knowledge of its location to you by word of mouth.

5 You walk over to the keepers of the tray and partake of their sushi.

Napster cocktail party

1 You enter at the foyer and the host of the party greets you. Around him are clustered thirty-five million of his closest friends.

2 Your only friend at the party is the host.

3 You would like to find the tray of sushi, so you find your way back to the foyer and ask the host where the tray has gone.

4 The host says, "Oh, yes, it's over there."

5 You hold the tray and choose your favorite sushi.

Source: Gnutella, by Gene Kan, from *Peer-to-peer*, edited by Andy Oram,
O'Reilly Publishing.

source programmer told online magazine *WiredNews*, "Bad code can be fixed, but conflicts and confusion among the coders themselves could stop the protocol that was supposed to be unstoppable ... Imagine that I ask you a question and you know that the answer is no. But instead of just telling me that, you proceed to ask everyone that you know what he or she thinks the answer is.

And they ask everyone they know … and on and on. That's the problem with a P2P network – there is no central authority that you can directly connect with who can supply the 'answer.' "

File sharing systems work best when there are enough users around for you to be able to share a critical mass of worthwhile files. That's why Napster kept growing and growing until it was effectively shut down. But as soon as a file sharing system has a critical mass, it's big enough to become a target of the lawyers acting on behalf of those whose copyright has been breached.

That's the dilemma: the attainment of popularity may signal the imminent demise of a service. Even so, one of the big problems for Napster was that it was centralized. By contrast, Gnutella can withstand a band of hungry lawyers. For a start it is nothing but a protocol; it's just freely accessible information. There is no company to sue and no one person is particularly responsible for it.

One downside of Gnutella is that while it is extremely flexible in this sense, when a search is performed, servers respond with an external IP address where the user can download the document, MP3 or whatever else it is. This means that Gnutella isn't the best for anonymity. And when a user logs out of the system, all of the files disappear as well.

Freenet

An Irishman created the original version of Freenet. Ian Clarke came up with it in his final year project in a degree in Artificial Intelligence and Computer Science at Edinburgh University, Scotland. The project was completed in June 1999 and Clarke made it available on the Internet, hoping that others would see its potential. His hopes were fulfilled and many took a keen interest.

What is Freenet? Well, it aims to create an information publication system similar to the World Wide Web, except with several major advantages. Information can be inserted into the system associated with a "key" (normally a description of the information such as "text/sport/football"). Anyone else can use the information if they use the right key. In one sense it is just like the World Wide Web, which requires a URL to retrieve a particular document. But unlike the World Wide Web, Freenet information is stored in a kind of central control in that it stores, catches and distributes the information based on demand. This allows Freenet to be more efficient at some functions than the Web.

There are differences between Gnutella and Freenet. They are often lumped together as the two decentralized alternatives to Napster and, like their more illustrious rival, they allow the sharing of MP3 files. But whereas Freenet is essentially all about sharing bandwidth and disk space with the goal of promoting free speech, Gnutella is a searching and discovery network that promotes free interpretation and response to queries. Freenet is optimized for computerized access to those files rather than human interaction.

Clarke is adamant that all Freenet implements is free speech and nothing more. Censorship is certainly an issue. It allows information to be published and read without fear of censorship because individual documents cannot be traced to their source or even to where they are physically stored. To participate in the Freenet system, users need to run a piece of server software on their computer and optionally use a client program to insert and remove information from the system.

What is interesting is that Freenet does not have any form of centralized control or administration. Because of this it will always be virtually impossible to forcibly remove a piece of information from Freenet. Furthermore, both authors and readers of information stored on this system may remain anonymous if they wish. Anyone can publish information because they don't need to buy a domain name or even a permanent Internet connection. Even more interestingly, the system has been arranged such that availability of information increases in proportion to the demand for that information. Information moves from parts of the Internet where it is in low demand to areas where demand is greater.

Yet sharing of copyright information is still a thorny issue. The Freenet network doesn't know the difference between public domain documents and work under copyright. It is perceived as a threat to traditional publishing and recording industries just as any other device that has made information sharing possible. All that Freenet does, say its developers, is share information more efficiently.

The Freenet Web site says it all: "While Freenet has the potential to assist copyright infringement, this battle has already been lost. Millions of copyrighted audio and video files are already being traded on the web each day and the absence of Freenet will not change that. Besides, by far the vast majority of copying activity does not take place online, but via old-fashioned, industrial-scale physical CD pressing."

Freenet therefore offers forms of anonymity, but while the decision to take down a file can be a personal decision by the publisher, there is a tendency for files not requested to sometimes drop off the system. There is a danger then that anything worthy but perhaps a little dull to many users may get shoved off the system.

Publius

There are other areas of potential for peer-to-peer systems. Publius is a Web-based publishing system designed to counteract censorship, which was set up by Marc Waldman, Lorrie Faith Cranor and Avi Rubin of AT&T Labs-Research.

A file published on the Publius system avoids being interfered with because it uses many different servers, so that no individual or organized group is likely to be able to destroy its content. One of the big problems with the Internet is that it is not that easy to use it completely anonymously. While this may not matter too much in a democratic society, dissent in other political systems can have harsh consequences for those who choose to protest.

The written word has always been a particularly powerful way of disseminating new and controversial ideas and the Internet has started to accelerate the process of word of mouth. Powerful ideas carry with them great danger for those who articulate them in an intolerant society, so intimidation of the author or authors of "dangerous" thinking usually follows unless anonymity can somehow be achieved.

The problem is that documents that are published have a URL that can be traced to a particular Internet host. If that host is in the pocket of the authorities then it can also be traced back to a particular file owner. The point about

Publius documents is that they can be read with a standard Web browser but still provide anonymity to those who post their thoughts online.

The point about the different servers is critical here. The servers are located all around the world and, crucially, they are all owned independently. They are owned and operated by volunteers and if one is shut down for whatever reason the others are there to provide back-ups.

As well as the server software, there is also software for interacting with the user. This gives a special proxy arrangement that asks a Web browser to publish files and retrieve them from others. Each user runs the proxy, either on their own computer or to that operating on the computer of someone else. The system seems to be very flexible – images, words and indeed any sort of file can be published with the Publius system. Published documents can be updated and deleted. The items can be anonymously published. Once the document is published there is no way to directly link the document to the publisher.

Publius is not a pure peer-to-peer, in that it may not require widespread holding of information at the PC end of the Internet system, but the deliberate dissemination of information among servers does give it some genuine peer-to-peer hallmarks. One particular strength of the Publius system is that is gives the publisher alone the right to improve or update material in a way that automatically directs anyone accidentally retrieving an earlier version of a file to the newer version. One other advantage is that it is one of the few file sharing systems that operate "above" the standard protocols for naming addresses on the Internet. On the plus side, this means that it can be used on a variety of operating systems with little in the way of modification. On the downside, this means that it is not as fast as it could be because it needs to use the protocol rather than allow a direct communication between a server and a Web browser.

Free Haven

There are some overlaps between the Publius system and that belonging to Free Haven, which is the brainchild of Roger Dingledine, Michael J. Freedman and David Molnar. The Free Haven project is devoted to designing a system of anonymous storage that resists the attempts of powerful adversaries to find or destroy any stored data. Its goals include anonymity for publishers, readers and servers. The publisher of the document determines its lifetime. It also has flexibility; the system is supposed to function smoothly as servers are added or remove themselves.

The Publius and Free Haven projects both address issues of how best to store files in order to preserve anonymity, but Publius in particular has no decentralized way in which to add new servers or get rid of existing servers. There is also no way in which to prevent publishers with a bee in their bonnet from filling up the system with just their views alone.

Both Free Haven and Publius are in a different bracket from other file sharing networks. The others, such as Gnutella, Freenet and Mojo Nation (of which more in Chapter 10) are those centered on the wants and needs of the readers. But Free Haven and Publius seek to concentrate on maintaining the anonymity of the publisher – once you add a file to the system it will be there forever should the publisher so wish. The downside is that because both are essentially storage networks, both are generally much slower to retrieve content from. Neither do they seem to handle the first idea that we gave of a perfect peer-to-peer system, that is, in which the system seems to cope well with lots of files and users switching onto and away from the system at any one point in time – something which Napster seems to cope with so brilliantly.

CONCLUSION

There are plenty of peer-to-peer systems around that compare in some way or another to that of Napster. Those like Gnutella and Freenet are essentially user focused, while those like Free Haven and Publius are much more to do with freedom of speech and preserving the anonymity of those who want to make their views more widely known, albeit at the expense of time and convenience. None of these systems on their own is going to make anybody very much money. But there would be fantastic possibilities if some way could be found to combine the user friendliness of the distribution system of Gnutella and Freenet, with the security conscious nature of the storage networks of Free Haven and Publius.

Potential commercial winners come from a variety of old and new economy backgrounds and represent many different types of application of peer-to-peer networking as defined earlier in this chapter. Which are the firms best placed to take advantage of this new format? Well there are companies such as Microsoft (with its .NET strategy) that are ideally placed to produce a business-to-business/peer-to-peer area in which to operate. Then there are the companies such as Groove Networks, who are bold startups in an exciting area with some really great ideas on making money out of it. There are also different forms of peer-to-peer developing, including distributed computing (where processing chores are broken up and sent out across a network of PCs), licensed media distribution companies, instant messaging frameworks, intelligent agents and mobile peer-to-peer networks

Among other beneficiaries of peer-to-peer networking are PC manufacturers and chip makers (such as Intel) who can see selling benefits in producing peer-to-peer facilities, software producers and Web sites that specialize in swapping, instant messaging and chat room facilities. Broadband providers are also in favor of file sharing because peer-to-peer boosts the value of broadband's unique selling point – its always-on connection. Certainly, the possibilities of the end user emerging as an information provider as well as a humble consumer will be good news for the likes of the DSL (digital subscriber lines) companies. These will be first in line to provide extra bandwidth alongside those companies able to provide dynamic Internet addresses. With power shifting to the individual because of Internet transactions, media businesses will also be amazed when passive consumers are replaced by millions of individualistic one-person media channels. The research group Forrester predicts that search engines such as Yahoo! and MSN will need to incorporate peer-to-peer searching by 2002 in order to satisfy demand from the growing number of users who want to be able to search the hard drives of willing users.

Who the major players will be is perhaps too soon to say, but it may be wise at this time to bet on the infrastructure players, those who are working on the ways to get much, much more out of underused PC hardware, than those who simply dress themselves up as peer-to-peer businesses, as if that were enough to help a company succeed as putting the label "e" ahead of your business name or ".com" after it seemed to be a guarantee of success at one point. These players are the subject of the next two chapters.

NOTE

1   "Listening to Napster", Chapter 2 of *Peer-to-peer*, edited by Andy Oram, O'Reilly Publishing.

CHAPTER 10

Newcomers and Old Stagers

INTRODUCTION

S UCH IS THE PROLIFERATION of peer-to-peer projects popping up all over the place that to pick out a few examples is very difficult indeed. In a young and rapidly developing area, trying to guess who is hot and who is not could be seen as a bit of a mug's game. And yet certain names keep cropping up when you look closely at the development of peer-to-peer business proposi- tions. They all subscribe to the same conceptual basis as Napster and other file sharing networks – the greater enjoyment for all through sharing, good intentions or the intention to share the burden of a collective project across resources. But they have very different ends to their more altruistic peers. All are set up with the intention, wholly or partly, of making money.

This chapter has been divided into three examples of three very different types of startups – Mojo Nation, Groove Networks and Living Systems – none of which existed more than five years ago. It also looks at the work done by three of what I have called old stagers – Microsoft, Intel and Sun Microsystems. In some senses it seems ridiculous to talk of these three as "old". Between them, these computing giants have less than 90 years of combined corporate wisdom – but in terms of the era of information technology, they are all very old indeed and made their highly profitable living well before the Internet became part of our everyday thoughts. Perhaps more importantly, all three still seem to have the agility to respond to the changing rules of the game brought about by the development of peer-to-peer systems, plus the financial clout to push their plans through.

NEWCOMERS

Mojo Nation

Mojo Nation adds a system of micropayments to the peer-to-peer file sharing debate. This means that somebody has to give something to a network to get something back.

Mojo Nation is, like Gnutella and Freenet and one or two others, a peer-driven content distribution technology. While other distribution frameworks like Napster or Gnutella may be sufficient to allow users to trade MP3 files, they are unable to scale up to deliver rich-media content while still taking advantages of the cost savings of peer-to-peer systems. Mojo Nation stores and delivers any kind of data – text, sounds, moving and still pictures, and other binary files. It claims to combine the flexibility of the marketplace with a "swarm distribution" mechanism to go far beyond any current file sharing system – providing high-speed downloads that run from multiple peers in parallel.

Most peer-to-peer content delivery relies on a single peer sending a requested file upstream. If that peer is overloaded, the requestor is probably out of luck. The idea behind Mojo Nation is that it breaks each uploaded file into small pieces, then replicates each small piece in several places over the network. When a user requests a file, Mojo Nation contacts a swarm of peers – rather than just one – before reassembling the file for delivery.

For Mojo Nation, every transaction costs some Mojo (the unit of currency on this system), and to acquire Mojo, one must contribute resources to the community. When demand for content is not great, the cost of providing that data is close to zero. When there is competing demand for that resource, then the payment system comes into play – Mojo Nation's distributed load system moves some clients to a less-occupied server, while other users have the option to use accumulated credit to move to the head of line.

The likes of Napster and Gnutella are built on the shifting sands of volunteerism. Freeloaders and parasites cannot be controlled. The freeloader gains all the benefit of the whole system and pushes the cost to those foolish enough to give away their resources. Xerox PARC researchers Eytan Adar and Bernardo A. Huberman documented these problems in their "Free Riding on Gnutella" paper that found 70% of Gnutella users provided no files or resources to the system and that 1% of the users were providing half of the total system resources.

This is a major obstacle to the successful working of such peer-to-peer systems. Peer-to-peer can save costs, but how can a content distributor encourage users to pitch in and help out? By giving credit where credit is due, say Mojo Nation. The Mojo Nation technology has an accounting mechanism built into the core protocols, ensuring that it is possible to keep track of those peers who have contributed services or resources to the network. This credit can be used as a form of karma within the system (e.g. "I provide a lot of resources to the system, so please move me to the front of the queue") or can be turned into real incentives by a licensee or third party. The accounting tool can also be used for royalty tracking and pay-per-view services.

The idea of getting something for something is very helpful in controlling things like denial of service attacks – if you have loads of requests from a single host you receive currency for each request. Only those with enough currency will be prepared to continue to bombard your machine.

Perhaps even more importantly for the future, the idea of micropayments of course allows you to engage in actual commerce through a file sharing network. If you want to trade content, micropayments allow people to send some currency to the producers of content as well as the servers.

Groove.net

Groove.net is the brainchild of Ray Ozzie, credited with inventing the e-mail and groupware system now known as Lotus Notes, the defining groupware product used by more than 60 million people worldwide. What does Groove do? Well, basically it's a better way of doing things than simply putting everything on the Internet for the purpose of sharing it. Groove.net combines elements of instant messaging and file sharing to offer a service for companies to install and develop.

Essentially, Groove.net is a bold attempt to create a new generation of knowledge management tools for business that brings the benefits of peer-to-peer file sharing to a closed community. Ozzie himself calls it "a platform for person-to-person collaboration with the spontaneity of e-mail." The most revolutionary aspect of the technology is that, in keeping with our parameters for peer-to-peer networking defined in Chapter 9, information will be shared via individual hard drives as opposed to corporate servers, which offers the hope of reducing the need for large amounts of bandwidth on a company network. Hence, Groove transforms not only the way you work but also the costs of traditional networks and maintenance.

Groove's software, named Transceiver, is a sophisticated affair. It includes all the tools a small group needs to interact. For a start, it allows users to communicate via text and voice, to share all kinds of files and to collaborate on, for instance, the editing of documents. The information in the documents can't be stolen either: in Groove, only those you invite see what you put in that space. It creates intelligent shared spaces that you define and into which you invite whoever you need and want to share information with, then encrypts the information, adds your digital signature and sends it to whoever you want.

This effectively creates a secure environment in which to invite other users of Groove to continue personal or business talk. Within the space in question, all information is stored on each user's computer and all changes are automatically updated on each others' machines.

The most interesting feature of Groove, though, is that it is effectively a kind of operating system for peer-to-peer computing, without the presence of a central server. The company hopes that other software firms will integrate their current systems with its new platform or write new applications for it. This will, in effect, create a computerized system similar to the sort that exists around Microsoft Windows.

Groove faces stiff competition from more established rivals (see later in this chapter). The Groove idea certainly seems to have taken off. By the beginning of 2001, Groove had signed up 100 partners in its first three months of operation. The partners signing on have all agreed to develop, deploy and support a variety of peer computing solutions for business use. Groove is clearly pleased with itself. Steve Wilkinson, vice-president of alliances at Groove Networks says, "We have been very pleased with the response and requests from software companies around the globe. They are eager to learn more about our peer computing platform and want to begin building Groove-based solutions that augment the Web and business process systems they've been developing for clients."

Groove's partners, mostly small companies, include BAE Systems, Full Moon Interactive, fusionOne, Perot Systems, STM Wireless and Zero Gravity Technologies. With lots of interest around it's interesting to hear opinions from one of them. Phil Stanhope, director of e-business alliances at Dallas-based Perot Systems told the online magazine *VarBusiness*,[1] "The Groove platform provides the basis for us to target key industries that are important to us: financial services, healthcare and logistics. These industries are driven by increasing regulatory and business requirements for secure and reliable, peer-to-peer communications ... Groove provides an opportunity to develop the next generation of applications and services for those industry segments."

Living Systems

Living Systems is a relatively undiscovered company. Its technology combines the notions of peer-to-peer networking with an understanding that markets need rules and transparency as well as free choice to operate effectively.

Founded in 1996 by Kurt Kammerer, now chief executive officer and Christian Dannegger, chief technical officer, Living Systems is in the rare situation of being a company in profit from day one. The company has focused on business-to-business aspects of file sharing long before anyone else. For example, in 1997, Living Systems worked on a joint research and development project with the German stock exchange.

The company's file sharing technology powers marketplaces, trading platforms and exchanges for a variety of industries such as agriculture, oil, media, financial services and logistics. Kammerer has been successful in positioning the company for leadership in this area. In his role as chief strategist and through his expertise in business-to-business markets, Mr Kammerer has been instrumental in designing and building B2B marketplaces in a variety of industries. As many big spending Internet ventures hit the wall, Living Systems serves as a reminder that thrifty business practices apply in the new economy.

HERE COME THE OLD STAGERS

If such startups fail to move into profit in the medium term, then commercial backers are likely to shift their gaze toward the efforts of major vendors such as Microsoft, Sun Microsystems, and Intel. Each, in their own way, is developing strategies for being at the front of the peer-to-peer networking revolution.

Microsoft and .NET

The fundamental idea behind Microsoft .NET is that the Internet itself becomes the basis of a new operating system, indeed, the platform for all computing in the future. This is a new distributed framework for creating, deploying, consuming, supporting and providing a development environment for Web services – a shift from individual Web sites or devices connected to the Internet, to constellations of computers, devices and services that work together (and intelligently) to deliver what Microsoft calls "broader, richer solutions." It not only makes Microsoft's earlier technologies easier to use, but helps Internet servers to divide the work up between themselves.

The so-called Hailstorm project, announced in the spring of 2001, is the first step in the translation of .NET from a vision into a reality. It represents the first generation of .NET-enabled Web services uniting and integrating previously separate islands of information on the Internet (today's Web sites and Windows applications). Hailstorm provides these islands with .NET interfaces, enabling them to communicate, inform each other of events and share data.

.NET is a project on which Microsoft is betting its house because it knows that if it doesn't go down this route, somebody else will. Unsurprisingly, vendors such as Microsoft have so much to lose from a server-less future that they are likely to spend significant sums just keeping up with peer-to-peer during the next few years.

In the first year of the 21st century, Microsoft invested more than $4 billion in research and development to advance its core businesses, build on its strategic investments and deliver on the promise of .NET, its most important software initiative ever. .NET is peer-to-peer writ large, a new era of empowerment for computer users at the edge of the Internet.

The reasoning of Microsoft is as follows. While using the Internet can be rewarding and a lot of fun, the different applications such as Web browsing, e-mail and contacts lists all have varying functionality and compatibility. Communicating between devices such as PCs, mobile phones and handheld PDAs is very difficult, while the sort of information that you would find on the Internet for each exist in isolation from each other.

The idea is that Microsoft .NET will allow isolated data and devices to communicate and collaborate more easily than at present. This it does by harnessing lots of different smart devices and Web sites with advanced software based on open Internet standards, such as XML. In other words, Microsoft .NET adapts to what the user is doing and how he or she is doing it and provides a universal interface for all of them.

In doing so, .NET has created tremendous potential for developers, says Microsoft, and this is where the peer-to-peer angle comes into play. It certainly is the logical route for Microsoft.

.NET builds on Microsoft's current core businesses, including the Windows family of desktop and server operating systems, enterprise server applications, Microsoft Office and MSN. Certainly, Windows 2000 is a powerful business operating system, the most powerful ever released by Microsoft and effectively forms the basis of Microsoft's .NET strategy.

Sun Microsystems

Already a leading provider of industrial strength hardware, software and services that help businesses make the most of the Internet, Sun Microsystems has also been getting in on the act. Since the foundation of the company in 1982, it has had one vision – "the network is the computer" – which seems very fitting in terms of our earlier definition of peer-to-peer.

In April 2001, Sun Microsystems unveiled Project Juxtapose (JXTA) as a prototype, "next generation" network computing research project that will enable easy peer-to-peer access on what Sun describes as the rapidly emerging multi-dimensional "expanded Web." Sun also launched jxta.org, an open source project where developers can collaborate and create innovative distributed services and applications that allow the users to quickly find, get and use information.

To help it along, Sun has bought Infrasearch, a provider of peer-to-peer searching technology. Infrasearch is currently developing a fully distributed peer-to-peer search engine which Sun says has the ability to return richer and more timely content on the Internet. Sun is banking that the addition of Infrasearch's technology to the JXTA efforts in peer-to-peer computing will address the network fundamentals of searching, sharing and storing information, which Sun believes is the key to harnessing the power of the Internet.

Sun Microsystem's slogan of the moment is "Find it. Get it. Use it." This means using it even if someone else has got it. Things have to be done this way say those at Sun, because the Internet is just getting too complicated to approach in any other way. "The Web is evolving in both depth and breadth into an 'expanded Web', which makes it challenging to efficiently communicate and access resources on the Internet," says Mike Clary, vice-president of Project JXTA. "Sun is offering a unified approach to address this next phase of distributed computing, an approach that will enable users to quickly find it, get it, use it."

Well he would say that wouldn't he? But all the same, the proliferation of content and resources moving online means that it is getting more and more time-consuming to naturally access information stored on multiple networks and across different platforms. Bill Joy, Sun's chief scientist and co-founder has no doubts: "Project JXTA fulfils a vision I have had for 25 years." He wanted all the strengths of technology generated by the likes of UNIX, Java and XML "so we started Project JXTA, which has become a platform independent, language agnostic open source technology to enable new and innovative distributed applications." Open source means that Sun has released the codes for JXTA (under license) to get everybody's best ideas on developing the software as quickly as possible.

Essentially, the peer-to-peer aspect of the JXTA project lies in the fact of the problem of finding, getting and using information and resources at the edge of the Internet. The technology allows users to make easier use of the Internet, harnessing its potential across many platforms. And for Sun it obviously means that people who find the Internet easier to use because of JXTA will come back to them for other things as well. For the average Internet user it means it will be much easier to find the information that he or she is really looking for without all the white noise of irrelevant results usually associated with trying to find things on the Internet. This can be done, say Sun, by having easy access to any peer or node on the network. JTXA will enable new applications that allow critical information to follow users across different network access points (such as mobiles and PDAs) so that the information is easily accessible and remains at users' fingertips.

Intel

Intel, meanwhile, has outlined an initiative to encourage the use of peer-to-peer technology in applications for sharing things like family videos, corporate documents and even network resources. Intel says it is looking to create what it calls a virtual private Web for companies or groups. Analysts believe that Intel has spotted the need for powerful chip technology at the desktop once more, and is backing peer-to-peer because it will help stimulate slumping chip sales.

In fact, Intel has been using peer-to-peer distributed computing technology since 1990. The compnay's NetBatch system links roughly 10,000 computers in a collective effort to design chips. The distributed computing architecture gives engineers access to a global network of processing power. "Within two years of implementing distributed computing, we eliminated new mainframe purchases and mothballed several we already had," says Pat Geisinger, vice president and chief technology officer of the Intel Architecture Group. To Gelsinger, peer-to-peer technology is yet another tool for bringing innovative solutions to complex network dilemmas: "Peer-to-peer is really the opportunity to use the Internet for its real, underlying architecture – an ad hoc, resilient, worldwide network of resources, all being able to directly communicate and interact with each other. To a great degree we're restoring the Internet to what it was built for."

Intel believes that peer-to-peer computing and all of the potential applications that go with it represent a shift in how the PC infrastructure will be used. Peer-to-peer technology, it says, is in a position to revolutionize

THE INTEL PHILANTHROPIC PEER-TO-PEER PROGRAM

Thousands of people are affected by cancer, diabetes, Parkinson's and other diseases. You don't have to be a scientist to help find a cure. The Intel philanthropic peer-to-peer program helps to combat life-threatening illnesses by linking millions of PCs into what it predicts to be the largest and fastest computing resource in history. This "virtual supercomputer" uses peer-to-peer technology to make unprecedented amounts of processing power available to medical researchers to accelerate the development of improved treatments and drugs that could potentially cure diseases. There's no cost to download and run the program and there's no noticeable impact on your computer's performance, because the program only makes use of the programming power that you are not using at any one moment in time.

computing environments and Intel processors such as the Intel Pentium IV processor mean, of course, that there is more power for its users to handle all the peer-to-peer tasks that Intel hopes they will want to take on.

Because of this potential commercial gain, Intel has been trying very hard to throw its weight around at the center of the debate by setting up working groups on peer-to-peer. It has come to the conclusion that peer-to-peer is about more than just the universal file sharing model popularized by Napster. This is what it says about the different business applications for peer-to-peer computing:

> *"Distributed computing and resources – peer-to-peer computing can help businesses with large-scale computer processing needs. Using a network of computers, peer-to-peer technology can use idle CPU MIPS and disk space, allowing businesses to distribute large computational jobs across multiple computers. In addition, results can be shared directly between participating peers. The combined power of previously untapped computational resources can easily surpass the normal available power of an enterprise system without distributed computing. The results are faster completion times and lower*

cost because the technology takes advantage of power available on client systems.

"Intelligent agents – peer-to-peer computing also allows computing networks to dynamically work together using intelligent agents. Agents reside on peer computers and communicate various kinds of information back and forth. Agents may also initiate tasks on behalf of other peer systems. For instance, intelligent agents can be used to prioritize tasks on a network, change traffic flow, search for files locally or determine anomalous behavior and stop it before it effects the network, such as a virus.

"Collaboration – peer-to-peer computing empowers individuals and teams to create and administer real-time and off-line collaboration areas in a variety of ways, whether administered, unadministered, across the Internet, or behind the firewall. Peer-to-peer collaboration tools also mean that teams have access to the freshest data. Collaboration increases productivity by decreasing the time for multiple reviews by project participants and allows teams in different geographic areas to work together. As with file sharing it can decrease network traffic by eliminating e-mail and decreases server storage needs by storing the project locally.

"Edge services – peer-to-peer computing can help businesses with large-scale computer processing needs. Using a network of computers, peer-to-peer can help businesses deliver services and capabilities more efficiently across diverse geographic boundaries. In essence, edge services move data closer to the point at which it is actually consumed acting as a network caching mechanism. For example, a company with sites in multiple continents needs to provide the same standard training across multiple continents using the Web. Instead of streaming the database for the training session on one central server located at the main site, the company can store the video on local clients, which act essentially as local database servers. It also utilizes existing storage space, thereby saving money by eliminating the need for local storage on servers."

These definitions from Intel help us to form the basis of our assessment of the best of the rest of the peer-to-peer businesses in the next chapter.

CONCLUSION

The six examples picked are only six of a large number of possible case studies, but hopefully highlight that the commercial potential of peer-to-peer extends well beyond the Napster concept of file sharing. At the core of all of the above examples is the notion of enlightened self-interest for all in sharing knowledge and/or resources. Mojo Nation adapted the Napster/Gnutella/Freenet model to take into account the need for some sort of micropayment in any commercial peer-to-peer system. Groove Networks showed the commercial potential for companies in installing and developing software not only for file sharing but also for instant messaging without the need for a central server. Living Systems the knock-on effect of file sharing for powering marketplaces, trading platforms and exchanges.

Microsoft's .NET project aims to simply make the Internet itself the operating system for a new powerful generation of computer users and devices operating and coordinating with each other at its edges. Sun Microsystems has always had the vision that "the network is the computer" and its vision is now becoming a reality, partly thanks to its own Project Juxtapose (JXTA), an open-source project which allows developers to talk to each other in developing new ways to access resources on the Internet. Finally, Intel is encouraging all sorts of peer-to-peer networks for one very good reason. Peer-to-peer means more power to the computer. More power to the computer means a demand for more (and more powerful) computers. This in turn means more processor chips sold. And guess who makes the chips?

NOTE

1   December 5, 2000, "Groove Networks links up with new partners."

CHAPTER 11

Irresistible Forces and Immovable Objects

INTRODUCTION

THIS CHAPTER LOOKS AT two types of companies that are making money out of peer-to-peer ways of doing business. The first group one could call the irresistible forces, examples of companies that are providing ways of using the essential elements of peer-to-peer. In Chapter 9 these were identified as being those that give the devices or people at the edge of the network a real level of autonomy and are flexible enough to allow the resources they hold to connect with one another in a highly unstable and rapidly changing environment. This is not just the file sharing of the Napster variety, seen also in the likes of Gnutella and Freenet, but ways of using peer-to-peer through, amongst other methods, distributed computing, distributed search engines and even mobile devices. At the basis of it all we see, as Shawn Fanning had hoped way back in Chapter 1, that people and businesses really do want to cooperate to get better results for everyone, be it in music or in business.

The second group could be labeled immovable objects. These are the companies making a mint out of preventing the abuse of copyright. This could be the subject of a book in itself, and someone is sure to tackle it in more detail than is allowed here. These companies are competing to develop watertight, unshakeable and immovable solutions to prevent copyright theft.

IRRESISTIBLE FORCES

Distributed computing

Distributed computing means that data chores are broken up and sent out to a network of PCs to be processed. In the days when processing chips were less

149

powerful, this was accomplished by a bank of PCs dedicated to the purpose. But thanks to the rapid increase in computing power, companies can now harness the power that currently resides on their employees' desktops, much of which is unused at any one time.

DataSynapse

Finance is a great area in which to demonstrate the power of distributed computing. DataSynapse was founded by two men familiar with the huge data processing requirements of the financial services industry. Chief executive Peter Lee was an investment banker at J P Morgan, while chief technical officer Jamie Bernardin worked in the advanced strategies and research group of Barclays Global Investors. Between them, the two came up with a product called WebProc, a peer-to-peer platform for distributing computer processes to idle and under-utilized resources. With this product it didn't matter whether the available resource was a server or a desktop PC – as long as it was connected to the enterprise's network in some way.

There is seemingly no downside to the employee of using processing power from his or her desktop. The solution is designed to integrate easily with the corporation's existing network environment and employees never notice when WebProc is working because it only takes control of a desktop PC when that PC is idle. Should a worker return to his desk during a computation, WebProc immediately interrupts the processing task and re-routes it to another idle system. The results of the DataSynapse WebProc solution are certainly impressive. Crunching complex derivatives contracts, for example, requires lots of power but for one retail bank, performance was improved by 80 times – whereas baseline time to process 200 trades on an existing server was 44 minutes, distributing those computations across 100 PCs meant that the job was finished in 33 seconds.

Completing such jobs faster is, of course, invaluable for a financial services company. It can boost the productivity of traders, allow a bank to react more swiftly to abrupt economic changes, and generally increase the number of trades a company can conduct. What's more, scaling such a system to handle more and more complex calculations is relatively simple.

Other examples of distributed computing

Applied Meta

Applied Meta (www.appliedmeta.com) is a new venture. It's early days, but it is looking to commercialize distributed computing technology that harnesses the full potential of networked computing resources. More specifically, Applied Meta has developed software that allows enterprises to effectively manage distributed systems – including networked servers, desktops and handheld devices across geographically dispersed locations.

Entropia

Entropia (www.entropia.com) is a provider of distributed computing, delivering supercomputer-scale power at low cost to accelerate computationally intense applications. Its Entropia 3000 distributed computing platform lets companies create a virtual supercomputer by using PCs they already own. The company says that this increases return on investment on their computers.

ePropose

ePropose (www.epropose.com) was founded in April 1999, to commercialize collaborative computing software. The software unites human interaction and process automation to deliver a new way to work – across people, systems, and firewalls.

Eyefrog

Eyefrog (www.eyefrog.com) is a privately held Californian company that is applying distributed computing solutions for network focused companies. Eyefrog's resource management system is a software package that makes the most of server resources. It also tracks usage and calculates resources on demand whenever required.

Improv Technologies, Inc.

Improv Technologies (www.improv-tech.com) is a software company using distributed computing for the management of digital services. Improv's Cirquet enables companies to centrally manage distributed services while reducing desktop maintenance, hardware, bandwidth, and application development costs.

NetSilica LLC

NetSilica LLC (www.netsilica.com) is focused on creating powerful business solutions through distributed computing. NetSilica's core application, the "enterprise peer network" (EPN), is designed to provide straightforward, secure, remote access to data and applications.

Uprizer

Uprizer (www.uprizer.com) is an emerging technology company that provides decentralized, distributed networking applications for businesses customers. Uprizer is co-founded by Ian Clarke, creator of the renowned Freenet (see Chapter 9).

WebV2 Inc.

WebV2's PeerBeans T product supports decentralized message handling and distributed business process execution (www.webv2.com).

Distributed search engines

Back in the old days, a single search engine was capable of grabbing every single document on the Web. Since then the Internet has simply got far too big. To adequately capture and catalog all the resources on the Internet, you'd need a computer as powerful as the Internet itself. So that's what distributed search engines do. They employ users' Internet-connected computers as a kind of distributed supercomputer that splits the job of spidering the Internet across thousands of individual boxes, each one doing what it can to aid the overall effort.

OpenCola

OpenCola (www.opencola.com) which was incorporated in 1999, is a distributed search engine. CIO Cory Doctorow explains what this means: "The traditional approach to Internet search is to create a searchable treasure-map, showing the location of every document online." In olden times, a single search engine was capable of grabbing every single document on the Web, visiting and revisiting each site to copy and index everything that got posted. Since then, Internet growth has accelerated the need for change. "Back then, the scale of the Internet was small enough that projects like Yahoo! seemed like a good idea: have a human being consider every new site online, review it, and add it to an hierarchical directory," says Doctorow, but according to Doctorow and his colleagues, that approach is no longer practical. "In the age of the billion-document Internet, human-mediated indexing projects are hopeless undertakings."

Even the traditional approach of using a single, monolithic server cluster to spider the whole Internet is laughable, says Doctorow. The millions of computers that comprise the Web cannot be matched by the power of a cluster of supercomputers.

OpenCola runs as a client and a server – a "clerver" – on your computer. When your computer is connected to the Internet, the clerver is in motion. The clerver has two jobs: finding documents and figuring out how to help other clervers. What really differentiates the search-engines is their intelligence, the degree to which they can evaluate the documents in their database and determine what – if anything – they're about. Doctorow says, "Clervers locate other clervers that are spidering the same sites as they are, negotiate among themselves to appoint a chief spider, which then breaks the spidering job up into little pieces."

According to Doctorow, effort aggregation is the key to OpenCola's methodology: "Clervers do more than identify, download and republish new documents from the Web. They do more than accept queries from other clervers about which documents in their cache match various relevant criteria – such as when my clerver says, 'Hey, you got any new documents from Wired.com that you think I'd like?" and your clerver replies with the URLs of three new Wired.com articles."

Doctorow says that clervers can serve as informational gurus: "Clervers also data-mine the queries that pass through them and play match-maker between users who have similar interests, passing each user's research methodologies around to similar users and allowing them to learn from one another.

This is effort aggregation at the lowest level: logging all the miniscule research decisions made by every user on the system, locating the users who have similar decisions to make, and giving them the benefit of other users' researches."

Plebio

Plebio is a search engine that searches all the online file databases on computers that run its software. The idea, the creation of Ashhar Farhan, a software writer from Hyderabad, India, is to create a peer-to-peer search network that will allow anyone to share any piece of information easily and quickly. Plebio can be used for whatever purpose the user intends, including commercial purposes, although the Plebio Web site points out that it only collects an e-mail address from the sharers, because the sole purpose of collecting the e-mail is to recover lost passwords for the sharers. Plebio software runs on the sharer's computers in such a way that it does not pass on any information about the sharer's computer apart from the list of file names within the shared folders.

Gonesilent.com

This company is building its peer-to-peer portfolio from the success of its previous incarnation as Infrasearch. Its main star is Marc Andreessen, the chairman and founder of technology company Loudcloud and former America Online chief technology officer. It's early days for Gonesilent.com, but the build up of Infrasearch provides grounds for encouragement. Sun Microsystems has recently bought it to become part of its Project Juxtapose (JXTA) which is one of the old stagers trying to tackle the peer-to-peer aspects of distributed computing (see Chapter 10).

Licenced distribution

Licenced distribution works like Napster file sharing technology, but for closed enterprise systems and (hopefully) minus the copyright infringement problems. It can also be used to facilitate work group collaborations between companies partnering on a project.

Kalepa Networks

Kalepa Networks (www.kalepa.com) provides content delivery and discovery technologies for distributed networks, using technologies such as file sharing, instant messaging, and Web services. Kalepa was founded by Miko Matsurmura, former Java technology evangelist and technical strategist at Sun Microsystems and a self-described "nerd."

Peer-to-peer, by definition, allows users to connect to computers over the Internet and share data and digital files, rather than having to access the information from a central server. So far, Kalepa has developed peer-to-peer software that works like Napster file sharing technology, but for closed enterprise systems and (it hopes) minus the copyright infringement issues. Kalepa is targeting its software to companies in four distinct markets: education, media, messaging, and storage. The software can also be used to facilitate work group collaborations between companies partnering on a project and the company plans to profit by licensing software and providing network services. The latter is akin to an application service provider model, which means Kalepa would maintain a customer's peer network environment for it.

That's only half the story. Kalepa is onto a much more ambitious project. Picture two concentric circles: an "outer edge" and an "inner edge" circle, says Matsurmura. The outer circle represents PCs – both in a public and private network system – that have downloaded Kalepa's software and can perform peer-to-peer functions. The inner circle – now under construction – would comprise network routers capable of coordinating both static and streaming (audio and video) content with the outer-edge circle of PCs. The idea is that the inner edge would assist the outer edge in running peer applications.

For example, if a PC on the outer edge gets 10,000 hits, the inner edge recognizes the overloads. It then uploads the desired application from the PC under siege, quickly coordinating its delivery to the 10,000 users so the public network isn't overloaded.

eMikolo Networks

Founded in 1999 and headquartered in New York with product development facilities in Israel, eMikolo Networks (www.emikolo.com) is the provider of what it calls an intelligent distribution network (IDN) technology that accelerates content distribution, lowers costs and improves performance of content delivery. eMikolo's demand driven access (DDA) software claims to be one of the only solutions that leverages the combined advantages of several technology areas – including content distribution and management, content routing and peer-to-peer – to optimize the use of bandwidth, thereby improving network performance and reducing costs.

Softwax

Softwax (www.softwax.com) develops and licenses peer-to-peer file sharing and content distribution technology to media companies, service providers and corporations. The Softwax system, once again, is a peer-to-peer file sharing network designed for lots of different sized companies and simple integration with existing software products, media distributors, ISPs and network infrastructure companies.

Messaging frameworks

Instant messaging is one of the success stories of mobile technologies. Designed on some mobiles as an afterthought, it has for many users, especially young ones, become the whole point of having a mobile. Now companies are starting to develop sophisticated commercial ventures within the instant messaging sector of peer-to-peer networking.

Jabber

Jabber (www.jabber.com) is an open source (i.e. being developed by lots of different people) project which combines instant messaging with a language known as XML. This language has usually been associated with making different transaction systems understand each other where businesses are dealing with other businesses. Jabber is not a single application but more of a glue that ties together people and services. It supports and even encourages the growth of diverse conversational systems.

From the start, Jabber was designed by a community rather than by any one individual, from peer-to-peer conversations. Although Jabber is open source, it allows a corporation or a service to manage its own namespace. It began in early 1998 out of a desire to create a truly open, distributed platform for instant messaging and to break free from the old fashioned centralized IM services.

One of the most important things to remember about Jabber is that its aim is to make conversations between people much, much easier. The idea, according to Jeremie Miller of Jabber, is to "create an open medium in which the user has choice and flexibility in the software used to manage conversations, instead of being hindered by the features provided by a closed commercial service. We hope to accelerate the development of peer applications built on an open foundation, by enabling them to have intelligent conversations with other people and applications and by providing a common underlying foundation that facilitates conversations and the accessibility of dynamic data from different services."

Intelligent agents

This is the development of technologies that allow collaboration to adopt "smarter" approaches to the management of shared information.

Consilient Inc.

The idea behind Consilient (www.consilient.com) is that a more intelligent approach to the creation, distribution and tracking of processes fosters greater collaboration throughout an enterprise and across its network of customers, suppliers, and partners. In so doing it uses its technology to transform the way in which companies do business. For example, the Consilient sitelet technology aggregates virtually any form of content – including documents, e-mail, Web pages, and application tasks and then distributes that content wherever, whenever, and however it is needed.

The core of its business focuses on solving four fundamental business challenges. It supports the so-called "real world" nature of business processes – the unpredictable combinations of manual and automated tasks that are distributed across multiple people, infrastructures and organizations. In so doing it makes its money from helping organizations to maximize the total value of their existing technology investments.

Other examples of collaboration

Engenia

Engenia (www.engenia.com) was founded in 1998 by Jeffrey Crigler, industry-acclaimed networking pioneer, and Jeffrey Kay, inventor of groundbreaking technologies for major companies, including IBM. Engenia's business is based around the potential of collaboration. Its technology empowers organizations throughout the value chain to sense and respond to changing business conditions, by enabling exchanges, extranets and extended enterprises to reap the rewards of collaboration between companies. Particular strengths include helping companies to achieve more efficient manufacturing, distribution and logistics.

Interbind

Interbind (www.interbind.com) says that its aim is to radically simplify and automate the creation, deployment and management of services offered on the Web. The whole point of business, they say, is to allow the seamless connection of all business data, applications and processes across the Internet within businesses and between businesses. The Internet offers a new degree of inter-program interaction that provides for the first time a way to build large, flexible applications dynamically from a set of standard independent software parts. The peer-to-peer aspect of all this is that Interbind's software allows business processes to move from disconnected systems to fully connected ones.

Mobile devices as peers

Mobile devices have proved popular for instant messaging between people, but there is also huge potential for shared information between the mobiles themselves. This is of particular interest for businesses that have large numbers of people on the move at any one time and are trying to develop corporate intranets.

Endeavors Technology

Endeavors Technology (www.endeavors.com) is a provider of Web-based peer-to-peer communication infrastructure with a core competence in enabling mobile devices to serve as information resources. Magi, deployable on desktops as well as mobile devices, links peers and includes messaging, presence management, and a bi-directional Web connection that facilitates file sharing and remote access.

iMulet.com

The iMulet.com company (www.imulet.com) harnesses the power of mobility to distributed computing technology. iMulet's products provide the basis for allowing digital content sharing, business and individual secure communication and collaboration and mobile instant messaging for 3G wireless networks.

IMMOVABLE OBJECTS

Digital rights management

Newton said that every action has a reaction and so it is in business. The subject of digital rights management could be a book in itself, but as the growth of file sharing and peer-to-peer communication as a business tool has become increasingly obvious, it is also clear that file sharing has a lot of businesses worried. Some are worried because the act of file sharing affects the security of their business systems, others because of the issues of copyright explained elsewhere in this book which are almost overwhelming in their complexity, and, finally, those who would somehow rather that file sharing didn't happen at all. Whatever the problem and the solution sought, it is clear that there is an awful lot of money to be made from this area of business. The rest of this chapter provides case studies of the key players developing digital rights solutions – the immovable objects that prevent the abuse of copyright that so many businesses dread.

How big will the digital rights management industry become? Answer – very big indeed. Stockbrokers J P Morgan have estimated that digital rights will be a boom area worth up to $273 million by 2003. Normally it is wise to treat such bandied about numbers with considerable caution and this may well be just one of the hundreds of Internet forecasts that predict so far ahead that nobody will remember the numbers when the time comes. But Peter Kumik, European managing director of Sealed Media, which sells digital rights management (DRM) software, is optimistic: "It may be wrong about the timescale, but personally I think that it's right in terms of value – perhaps just a couple of years early."

Digital rights management (DRM) ensures that the owner of the rights is paid for usage. DRM can be applied to books, pictures, music and video, and also to designs, proposals and business plans. Encryption is essential to DRM and the recent availability of so-called "strong" encryption has allowed an explosion in the number of suppliers. It has also generated middlemen, the clearing houses, which handle the digital rights purchases and licenses on behalf of publishers, tracking usage and ensuring that everyone gets paid. Just as there is fierce competition amongst DRM companies, so there is in clearing houses, where the top names include Magex, Reciprocal, Supertracks and DigiHub. One key problem that all DRM companies have to struggle with is the "user experience." While people are used to downloading files, they are unused to the fences that DRM puts around using them. All DRM companies agree that whoever gives the best user experience will gain significant market share.

Ian West, European vice-chairman of the DRM company Intertrust explains that it's a big mistake to think that consumers are the only ones who will be affected by the rise of online rights management – and an even bigger one to think it's only about music and videos. "Music is the target for DRM companies mostly at the moment, because of Napster and the present narrowband nature of most of the Internet. Video will be next – the executives at film companies are about to get some big whacks around the head the way that the music industry did. I can rip a DVD now and send it to 50,000 friends. A Napster for films? It already exists." (See Chapter 8.)

But there's a very important business-to-business element too, says West: "Say that I'm sending you a terms sheet of how I want us to do business, something written only for you, and that I didn't want you to pass it on to

HOW DIGITAL WATERMARKS WORK

One form of digital rights management is the equivalent of the security line on an English sterling note. A digital watermark is created by an ongoing pattern of digital messages that can be detected by computers but not by the human ear. The messages continue throughout the song so that even if you play an MP3 for less than a second, all the information in the watermark is obtainable. The mark contains a copyright holder as well as a serial number that uniquely identifies it. The watermark is encrypted and removing it is impossible without destroying the sound quality. Bots – software agents that work without direct supervision – scour the Net then track the progress of unauthorized distribution.

A common form of copyright protection uses two watermarks: one strong and the other weak. The strong watermark survives a song being converted into MP3 format. The weak watermark, on the other hand, is destroyed by the compression process. An SDMI (secure digital music initiative – the common watermark plan enacted by record labels and electronics manufacturers) compliant device looking for the strong watermark would then know to look for the weak one. If the weak one could not be found, the device would know it was a copy.

my competitors. I could set up the digital rights so that you can't print it and can't forward it from your computer. The whole B2B application can apply to anything to do with purchasing which enables a specific purchaser to approve specific uses of digital goods such as documents. In many ways, B2B is the biggest market, but less sexy than the consumer one. It's the music side which gets all the analysts' attention."[1]

With so much money in the digital rights market, it's no surprise that there is so much jostling for position. Rick Fleischman, senior director of evangelism at Liquid Audio, which provides DRM principally for music says, "The standards are getting set now that will end up being the reality for a long time to come." The principal standard being fought over is whether you should be tied to one computer or platform to use your rights, or whether you have to be online to validate those rights. Intertrust, for example, uses the untethered model, where you store the license on your computer and can buy more rights offline; the purchase is then put into a sealed software "box" on the computer and validated the next time you go online. By contrast, the "tethered" model favored by Microsoft, IBM, Xerox and Sealed Media ties you to being online when you use the license. This allows for centralized license storage and security and does have the benefit that you don't have to be on "your" computer to use a digital rights managed product which you had on another machine.

There are so many DRM providers springing up that it is only possible here to provide a few examples of the other leading players in the market.

"Hunters" in the DRM stakes: Envisional Software

"What we have is the best technology in the world. And that's a fact." CEO Ben Coppin and his colleagues at Envisional Software don't come up short in the confidence stakes. To understand why Coppin and his team of twenty or so Cambridge-based upstarts are so sure of themselves you have to look at who is now relying on them. Around the time of officially launching their company in the autumn of 2000, their services were snapped up by the International Federation of the Phonographic Industry (IFPI), which represents the intellectual property rights of the music industry. So far the signs are good: Envisional's search engine technology is enhancing the ability of major players in the music industry to protect their intellectual property from Internet pirates, which causes an estimated £1 billion loss in revenue each year.

Envisional is offering something which goes a step beyond existing software. Traditional search engines are fine for finding lots of things but have been unable to provide any real precision in the way that information is retrieved, making it very difficult, expensive and time consuming for large organizations to monitor brand abuse and the theft of intellectual property over the Internet. When it comes to the level of detail that companies require to monitor copyright abuses, says Coppin, existing search technologies are simply not up to the task: "If you use a search engine to find places where someone is misrepresenting your brand, you could be at it all day, or all year. Very difficult task."

Envisional's software, the "discovery engine," filters and categorizes information with a new level of accuracy, providing in-depth and targeted knowledge of information published on the Internet. How? They came up with a way in which a machine could effectively allow the user to put in a lot of expert knowledge about their brand or copyright material. "As well as power, which all search engines need," says Coppin, "we have flexibility." Flexibility is the key selling point for Envisional because a normal search engine tends to be at the low end of a flexibility scale.

This means that Envisional can sell to lots of different types of companies. Coppin says, "Doing protection for one type of company is very different from doing it for another company. If you have a search engine that looks for MP3 files it may not be very good in locating brand abuse. We can do both." With the IFPI already in the bag, Envisional has several other big deals in the pipeline and has impressive expansion plans and healthy backing, and Coppin had good reason for feeling confident.

The DRM managers: Madge.web

J.P. Bommel, vice-president of digital music for Madge.web, (www.madge.com) is in a good position to help the music industry in its struggle over the nightmare issue of intellectual property rights and distribution. Launched in Cannes in January 2001, Bommel claims the digital music division is the only organization that can provide the music industry with digital music hosting and distribution services at a truly international level. "Napster is undoubtedly the best application for the music industry today," he says. "We have essentially built a legal form of Napster."

The company helps businesses to maximize their assets with what it calls rich Web content. The rationale is that, in future, Web content will not consist of simply text and the odd picture. Indeed it will go beyond on-demand content such as video clips to encompass content distribution. "Napster gave everyone in the music industry a wake-up call," says Bommel. "But our research shows that if we give people good files with no viruses they would be more than willing to pay a little bit for them. Madge.web tries to connect the artist with the fan so its target market is the record labels, the artist community and, of course, the retailers. The solution is secure and we control it over our network."

KEY DIGITAL RIGHTS MANAGEMENT PLAYERS
Microsoft

Windows Media Player (www.microsoft.com/uk) now includes compressed data for playing DRM protected songs. It is also used for rights protected videos by companies such as newsplayer.com, which offers video clips from the past century. It uses online validation method for licenses, making unlicensed distribution impossible. More than 100 million (free) licensed copies of Windows Media Player have been distributed or downloaded.

Liquid Audio

Liquid Audio (www.liquidaudio.com) was formed in January 1996 in California. It is making inroads to the music industry and expects to realize $27 billion from online sales over the next three years – if Napster can be quelled. Liquid Audio has a deal with Napster which could allow songs that are downloaded from the site (rather than swapped with others) to be decoded only with purchased licenses. Traded on Nasdaq (LQID), it has more than 750 affiliate Web sites.

Intertrust

Ten years old and listed on Nasdaq since 2000, Intertrust (www.intertrust.com) is a major player in DRM that hustles into deals amidst much bigger companies. The company provides an end-to-end DRM solution that creates a local database that stores the user's rights, identities, transactions, budgets and keys. A key client is Bertelsmann Music Group.

Sealed Media

Originally British but now based in the US, Sealed Media (www.sealedmedia.com) was founded in 1996, and has since grown to employ nearly 50 people. Aimed largely at the publishing market, with PDFs, HTML, images and video its main diet, the software prevents screen grabbing of rights-protected files – which was a major weakness in the protection around Stephen King's e-book.

IBM

IBM's Electronic Media Management System (EMMS) (www.4ibm.com/software) is initially aimed at music and audio content and was tested in a broadband trial with the five biggest record companies last year. It major components include a content mastering system, tools for hosting music content and promotional materials and tools for online music retailers supporting the sale of digital music to consumers. The system also incorporates its own clearing house, which tracks the sale of digital music content, and manages access and usage privileges as designated by the original music owner.

PassEdge

PassEdge (www.passedge.com) is a startup based in Oregon, which has developed DRM for streaming video, aimed at what it sees as the potential $132 billion online video market. Called StreamAccess, the product encrypts at the Internet connection level and independent of the application being used to view the video; it verifies the user via an online digital certificate. This means that users' rights can be changed during a stream, leading to improved control of access by the streaming company than at present, where streams run with little control.

NOTE

1   See Charles Arthur, "Digital Rights Management," *Internet Business*, September 2000.

CHAPTER 12

Conclusion – Napster, Business and the Future

S HAWN FANNING DIDN'T INVENT FILE SHARING. He didn't invent the concept of peer-to-peer networking. And he didn't even invent Napster totally on his own. It was his idea of course and mostly his frenzied efforts that saw Napster from the drawing board onto millions of desktops around the world, but he needed all the help he could get from those around him in moments when he thought he had hit a brick wall.

Perhaps it is appropriate that this young man was so prepared to benefit from the wisdom of others, accept their advice and share around the phenomenal workload involved in writing the Napster software and server programs. He developed his dream by sharing it with others, in much the same way that those who use or have used Napster shared their MP3s.

It is really important to remember that Shawn Fanning's achievement has been based around the positive experiences of sharing information and viewpoints. Almost everything he learnt about computers came from one of two sources. Work colleagues at his uncle's company taught him a lot about programming and later he became a regular visitor to Internet chat rooms where he picked up the technical mastery that only more experienced software developers could pass on. His experiences told him that music file sharing was not only possible but highly desirable. A friend who knew Fanning at the time says that he's pretty sure that Fanning just woke up with the idea one day that "it would be neat if people could share their music with one another." Fanning believed (and perhaps only a teenager could be idealistic enough to have such a vision) that people would actually love to share unconditionally what was theirs with one another and chat to each other about their favorite types of music.

Fanning found plenty of help from underground hacker groups to deal with the technical issues, but he soon found himself meeting people who told him that his program would never become popular because people would simply not be interested in a file sharing program. One hacker even said, "it's a selfish world and nobody wants to share." Yet Fanning's thoughts were much more sanguine about human nature: even selfish people would be up for sharing, if only through enlightened self-interest. The feeling drove him on ... and on. Friends believe that he was driven to develop Napster mainly through a desire to prove to himself and others that human nature was not intrinsically selfish.

Fanning's passion for Napster became infectious. Jordan Ritter, one of those who helped Fanning develop the Napster program and server recalls 50-hour shifts of pumping code, fuelled only by Red Bull and pizza. The product that emerged was quite simply, like so many brilliant things, simple, clean and easy to use, yet awe-inspiringly powerful. Napster had no marketing budget, no advertising behind it, and yet in retrospect it seems obvious that word of Napster would spread across the world like wildfire.

Yet retrospect is a wonderful thing. At the time of course it took everybody, especially those who had doubted the appeal of file sharing, by surprise. Anyone who has received a humorous joke by e-mail and forwarded it to a friend or colleague, only to be told, "Oh yes, I've only received that one three times already today" will know all about the power of critical mass. Forward the joke to ten friends who forward to ten friends and you've got the joke coming back to you quicker than you can say "viral marketing." Napster's reputation spread quickly and the more quickly it spread the more people checked it out. And the more that people checked it out, the bigger the range of available MP3s. And the bigger the range, the more that people liked Napster and the more that people liked Napster, the more quickly its reputation spread. And so on and so on.

One estimate of Napster users, just before a court ordered it to remove all materials subject to copyright infringement, put the figure at around 58 million. Nobody really knows if this is totally correct, but then all you really need to know when the numbers get that big is that we're talking about an awful lot of people from all walks of life. Their sheer numbers also removed any guilt they may have felt about copyright infringements – if they felt any guilt at all. The truth is that psychologically most people don't see themselves as breaking the law by downloading MP3s anonymously in their own home on their own computer. Napster made guilt-free crime possible *en masse*. Certainly, people have no problem at all in breaking laws whose only purpose at first sight seems to enrich corporate lawyers ahead of other artists and performers.

As well as consumers, the success of Napster has also made many business people sit up and take notice. Unfortunately for Napster, most of those noticing initially came from record labels, their representative trade bodies and a collection of big name artists, all very angry indeed that the spread of Napster, which had at first been ignored, was leading to the mass breach of copyright. The irresistible forces of peer-to-peer networking had suddenly come up against the establishment's immovable objection to breaking the law. Why should everyone get so upset? Edward Rothstein, writing in the *New York Times* perhaps put it most eloquently when he wrote, "Information doesn't want to be free; only the transmission of information wants to be free. Information, like culture, is the result of a labor and devotion, investment and risk; it has a value. And nothing will lead to a more deafening cultural silence than ignoring that value and celebrating ... [companies like] Napster running amok."

Of course, not many in the record companies saw the arguments in quite such a sophisticated way. Put bluntly, as far as the major labels were concerned, Napster users were robbing them blind. The base motivations of Vivendi *et al* were a combination of fear, indignation and desperate self-preservation in the face of Napster's phenomenal popularity. The malcontents consisted of the five global record companies (at the time of writing, mergers between various of the five are being mooted, dismissed and resurrected), fronted by the Record Industry Association of America's Hilary Rosen (described by one music artist in this book as "a lioness defending five cowards"). Then there were the big name artists like Lars Ulrich of Metallica. Ulrich took a considerable amount of flak from music lovers for suggesting that not only should he be paid for his music but that he should be reimbursed the cost of studio time and the like in developing and promoting his work.

The record industry, of course, won the battle over copyright. But in taking action against a service so phenomenally popular, it made the industry status quo impossible to maintain. In terms of its relationship with the fans, the lawsuit served only to raise awareness of Napster. Once people saw the file sharing potential of Napster through millions and millions of people logging on, people became aware of their collective power. People in their millions, some stirred into interest only by the controversy over copyright, loved the music to which Napster had given them access, the feeling of community it generated and the sense of empowerment that it gave them over big business. Their wrath over Napster's targeting by big business unleashed a wave of fury through the underground Internet, via chat forums throughout the online world.

These opinions in turn have helped to shape the attitudes of artists and record companies. The former have become more aware of a possible direct connection with their fans through the Internet in a way which could ultimately cut out record companies altogether. The record companies for their part now recognize that Napster was a phenomenal success, in part because the technology already exists to make MP3 downloads an easy and convenient aspect to the music collections of most fans. If that's what the fans want, then it has become inevitable that that is what the fans will get, with or without the major record labels.

Of the major record labels, Bertelsmann is perhaps the most enlightened of a pretty bad bunch. It has of course now teamed up with Napster to produce a subscription service but there are some very real doubts as to whether Bertelsmann or its peers have the wherewithal to make a subscription service work. Ultimately it's very difficult to sell expensive beer in a free bar and the proliferation of other music file services and networks means that there is plenty of free (or at least cheap) music to be found on the Internet for those who know where to look. Similar trends are showing elsewhere. The panic caused by Napster in the record industry has already been replicated with the punishment and closure of the Scour network through the courts at the behest of the movie industry.

Nevertherless, the fact that Bertelsmann and Napster were able to make a deal shook two worlds: it shook the world of Napster users, who suddenly worried whether life would be as much fun from now on, but it shook the business community into assessing the commercial potential of peer-to-peer networking. And this is the point at which one has to become very careful about what peer-to-peer actually means. As this book has made clear, the trouble with the label peer-to-peer is that it is currently an immature buzzword. Some people say it's simply people or things communicating directly with each other. End of story? Well peer-to-peer includes these actions (such as talking on the telephone) but is really much, much more.

For example, Napster involves direct communication between peers but relies heavily on a central server for listings. But Napster is the whole reason that the debate over peer-to-peer has taken off and so a wider definition has been used in this book. Whatever happens to Napster in the long term, the reality is that it has proved itself to be an outstanding example of success in the peer-to-peer revolution and can't simply be ignored. Therefore our definition of peer-to-peer has to specify whether this or that example gives the devices or people at the edge of the network a real level of autonomy. Secondly, the subject has to be flexible enough to allow the resources they hold to connect with one another in a highly unstable and rapidly changing environment. Napster scores heavily on both counts.

The really important thing to remember about the potential of Napster is that it was created in order to solve the problem faced by Shawn Fanning's roommate. The technological solutions had a purpose – someone had actually requested it. People wanted something like Napster – so Fanning did his best to come up with the goods. It is a rare example of supply matching demand in technology, which is why Napster simply cannot be ignored. Usually supply comes first and then its creators wonder why the general public isn't smart enough to understand its potential. Suppliers often whine that the public doesn't understand their product or service and "needs educating" but at the end of the day the public will buy only those things that improve the quality of their lives, or save them time or money.

As Napster has become embroiled in legal battles, those interested in file sharing have begun to explore other file sharing systems. Decentralized systems like Gnutella, Freenet, Publius and Free Haven move us on in understanding the potential of peer-to-peer but because they in no way provide a basis for a commercial utopia, none of these systems in themselves is going to make anybody very much money. But they do provide an important platform on which to build commercial applications. New players such as MojoNation, Groove Networks and Living Systems and old stagers such as Microsoft and Sun Microsystems are now emerging which do have commercial potential.

Among other beneficiaries of peer-to-peer networking are PC manufac-turers and chip makers (such as Intel) who can see selling benefits in produc-ing peer-to-peer facilities, plus software producers and Web sites that special-ize in swapping, instant messaging and chat room facilities. There are also different forms of peer-to-peer developing, including distributed computing (where processing chores are broken up and sent out across a network of PCs), licensed media distribution companies, instant messaging frameworks and mobile peer-to-peer networks. Then, to find all these things involves the need for distributed search engines. The research group Forrester predicts that search engines such as Yahoo! and MSN will need to incorporate peer-to-peer searching by 2002 in order to satisfy demand from the growing number of users who want to be able to search the hard drives of willing users.

Broadband providers are also beneficiaries from peer-to-peer because it boosts the value of broadband's unique selling point, which is of course its always-on connection. Certainly, the possibilities of the end user emerging as an information provider as well as a humble consumer will be good news for the likes of the DSL (digital subscriber lines) companies. These will be first in line to provide extra bandwidth alongside those companies able to provide dynamic Internet addresses. With power shifting to the individual because of Internet transactions, media businesses feel challenged when passive con-sumers are replaced by millions of individualistic one-person media chan-nels.

Who the major players will be is perhaps too soon to say, but it may be wise at this time to bet on the infrastructure players, those who are working on the ways to get much, much more out of underused PC hardware. Much better to put your money on these rather than those who simply dress themselves up as "peer-to-peer" businesses, as if that were enough to help a company suc-ceed. We should know by now that putting the label "e" ahead of your business name or ".com" after it is no guarantee of success.

Although Shawn Fanning didn't invent file sharing or the wider concept of peer-to-peer networking, he inspired the development and debate over both. His achievement in creating Napster is the living embodiment of an enlight-ened "sharing" culture that is sweeping the world of business only five years on from the moment his uncle bought him his first computer. Even if Napster itself fades into obscurity, as it well might, the legacy of sharing has already started to reshape the business world.

Index